2440 QUESTIONS and ANSWERS

2440 QUESTIONS and ANSWERS

ENTERTAINING, ENTICING, AND ERUDITE ENTRIES FROM A TO Z GUARANTEED TO TICKLE YOUR CEREBELLUM

FRED B. WRIXON

Arlington House
New York

Published 1985 by Arlington House Inc.
distributed by Crown Publishers, Inc., 225 Park Avenue South,
New York, New York 10003

Printed and bound in the United States of America

Library of Congress Cataloging-in-Publication Data
Wrixon, Fred B.
2440 questions and answers.
Bibliography: p.
1. Questions and answers. I. Title. II. Title: Two thousand four hundred forty questions and answers.
AG195.W79 1985 031'.02 85-15736
ISBN 0-517-49475-2

h g f e d c b a

TO MY FAMILY

CONTENTS

2440 QUESTIONS and ANSWERS

INTRODUCTION

Welcome to the world of often teasing, sometimes tricky, but always fascinating facts!

Among the 2440 questions and answers contained in this book, you will find entertaining, enticing, and erudite entries from A to Z. There are curios for the curious, puzzles for party guests, and mind games for mentalists.

The contents, however, are much more than a collection of random knowledge. Each of the topics is alphabetically arranged for easy access. The questions are structured in levels of difficulty from the better known to the more obscure. This progression is as follows: 1 and 2 are relatively easy; 3, 4, and 5 are moderately vexing; 6 to 10 are more difficult.

This book has been arranged to be played as a complete quiz game for one or more. You choose the topics and assign the points. There are multiple-choice matches and a chance to pick true or false answers. You can race a stopwatch or enjoy each page at your leisure.

Speaking of watches, the seconds are passing. Why not turn to one of your favorite categories and try a few questions? There's no time like the present to begin!

ALPHA

This is the beginning of our journey along the many-forked Trivia Trail. Alpha begins with the letter A; also, it is the first letter of the Greek alphabet. So, let's get started!

1. The biblical "Father of Nations," he is revered by Christians, Moslems, and Jews alike.

2. Tangiers and Tanzania are on this continent.

3. What word describes either an apparatus for shaking or a person who tries to arouse dissatisfaction with the status quo?

4. An albino member of the world's largest mammal family led this tormented seaman to his doom. What was the seaman's name?

5. This king of the Visigoths is rarely remembered for his unusual feat of conquering Rome in A.D. 410.

6. This ancient Greek capital of Egypt was also the site of the famous Pharos lighthouse.

7. Who wrote the popular series called the *Alger Books* for boys?

8. Which palace of thirteenth-century Moorish kings is now a site of artistic splendor in Spain?

9. If your secretary wants a new title and takes dictation, you can call him or her by this name and still be quite right.

10. What term describes the attributing of human characteristics to everything from gods to trees and mountains?

ALPHA

answers

1. Abraham. He is regarded as a patriarch by a number of nations in the Middle East and in other parts of the world.

2. Africa.

3. An agitator.

4. Captain Ahab of Herman Melville's *Moby Dick.*

5. Alaric (A.D. 370?–410). He is often confused with the Hun leader Attila (A.D. 406?–453).

6. Alexandria. The lighthouse was one of the Seven Wonders of the World.

7. Horatio Alger, an American writer of inspiring tales of young people's achievements.

8. The Alhambra. (Arabic: *al hambrā*, the red house). It is located near Granada, Spain.

9. An amanuensis. (Latin: *manu,* hand + *ensis,* relating to).

10. Anthropomorphism. (Greek: *anthropo*, man + *morphic*, having a form). This technique is often used in prose and poetry.

AMERICAN HISTORY

Our nation's history is filled with countless curiosities. Put on your tricornered thinking cap to recall these facts about our unique past.

1. This hero of the Battle of Saratoga became a traitor because of his misguided pride and greed.

2. Which state was the first to give formal sanction to the constitution, thus gaining the name First State?

3. She was the first English child born in America, yet her entire life remains a mystery.

4. Who used a half moon and one discovery to find two historically imporant bodies of water?

5. What was the Constitution of the original thirteen colonies called?

6. This region was called Deserette when its settlers first applied for statehood in 1849.

7. What was the name given to New England's Pilgrims when they sought independence from the powerful Church of England?

8. A wise and capable Colonial leader, he could never be President because of the place of his birth.

9. Which early suffragette wrote the theme song of the Union Army during the American Civil War?

10. Which state was formed by "reverse rebels" during the War Between the States (1861–1865)?

AMERICAN HISTORY

answers

1. Benedict Arnold. A statue was raised in honor of his heroism in Saratoga, New York. However, the name was removed after his treachery at West Point.

2. Delaware has that honor.

3. Virginia Dare. Virginia, her parents, and the entire Roanoke Island Colony disappeared without a trace in 1587–1588.

4. English explorer Henry Hudson. His ships, *Half Moon* and *Discovery*, were instrumental in his exploring both the river and bay bearing his name. However, Estevan Gomez, a Portuguese explorer, now is credited as being the first to find these bodies of water. He entered what became New York's harbor area in 1525. Hudson did not arrive until 1609.

5. The Articles of Confederation (1781–1788).

6. Deserette eventually became Utah. The largely Mormon founders transformed a virtual desert into a verdant, productive state.

7. The Puritans. They wanted to reform, or "purify," the elaborate ceremonies of the Church of England.

8. Alexander Hamilton. His birth on the island of Montserrat in the West Indies made him ineligible for the presidency.

9. Julia Ward Howe. Her classic "Battle Hymn of the Republic" was a popular and patriotic campfire song.

10. West Virginia. Families in the mountainous western sections of Virginia chose to secede from the rebellious state of Virginia and became "reverse rebels."

ANCIENT HISTORY

This won't be boring. Remember how popular King Tut's treasure tour was? The ancients did lead fascinating lives. See if you can decipher these secrets of the ages.

1. He was an emperor who occupied himself strangely while his city burned.

2. According to legend, this "giant" statue, an ancient wonder, stood astride the harbor of the Dodecanesean island for which it is named.

3. She ruled a great empire as the last of the Ptolemaics.

4. Can you name the landmarks known as the Pillars of Hercules that were once considered to be the world's edge?

5. This Roman general, one of the first "guerrilla" fighters, defeated the seemingly invincible Hannibal through a series of surprise attacks and maneuvers.

6. This conqueror cut a knot that he could not untie and rode a horse whose Latin name meant ox-headed. Identify him and his steed.

7. Which Greek cynic philosopher garbed himself in a curious costume to search for an honest man?

8. Whose "victory" at Asculum in 279 B.C. will always be remembered as too costly and thus no victory at all? *Clue:* Asculum is now the town of Ascoli Satriano in southern Italy.

9. What was the unusual "wall of wood" that an oracle predicted would help the Greeks defeat the Persians in the year 480 B.C.?

10. Though called a witch by some, this brave heroine led a revolt of Britons against Roman rule.

ANCIENT HISTORY

answers

1. Nero Claudius Caesar Drusus Germanicus. Yes, that was his full name. He was reputedly cruel and depraved. But whatever he was doing when Rome burned, he certainly wasn't "fiddling," for the fiddle hadn't been invented yet.

2. The Colossus of Rhodes. Dedicated to Apollo, it was a huge work of art. However, the architecture of that day (280 B.C.) was not advanced enough to permit an object to stand astride a harbor.

3. Cleopatra.

4. Gibraltar in Spain, and Jebal Musa, the lesser-known mountain, in northern Morocco.

5. Scipio Africanus.

6. Alexander the Great and his horse Bucephalus. Legend says that Alexander cut the special knot tied by King Gordius of Phrygia. This was the sign that Alexander would be Asia's master.

7. Diogenes. He supposedly was attired only in a barrel and carried a lantern in search of an honest man.

8. Pyrrhus, king of Epirus. He lost so many men at Asculum that his success was hollow. All such "victories" are pyrrhic.

9. The "wall" was a fleet of wooden ships by which the Greeks won the battle of Salamis Bay.

10. Boadicea. According to the Roman historian Tacitus, she united several villages in a courageous but unsuccessful attempt to expel the Romans.

ANIMALS

We all have some awareness of the animal kingdom through pets, stories, or movie favorites. However, did you know . . .

1. What is the smallest dog, named after a state of Mexico?
2. What is the name of the bullfrog in Three Dog Night's song "Joy to the World"?
3. What is a drake to a duck and a gander to a goose?
4. In the *Thin Man* movie series, what was the name of the Charleses' dog?
5. To early Africans it was the camelopard. To us, what is it?
6. If you know the 1940s slang for pretty legs, you can give another name for a herd of whales.
7. Can you name the only cat without a tail?
8. What little-known yet visible features give a bloodhound its keen sense of smell?
9. What is the only species of deer in which both sexes have antlers?
10. He was the Vitagraph dog in 1911—the first animal "star."

ANIMALS

answers

1. Chihuahua.

2. Jeremiah.

3. They both are of the male gender.

4. Asta.

5. The giraffe. It once was mistaken for a cross between a camel and a leopard.

6. The word is gam. Gams are a pair of shapely appendages.

7. The manx. It is believed to have originated as a type of mutation on the Isle of Man in the Irish Sea.

8. The wrinkled layers of the bloodhound's facial skin. These folds help to trap and hold the various scents.

9. The caribou. It is a variety of reindeer.

10. Gene. Sorry, Morris, but he had his name in lights long before you.

VISUAL QUIZ NUMBER ONE

ARDOIS

ARDOIS

The Ardois signal system is used to send visual messages at sea with red and white electric lights. Here it is presented as one of several communications systems for solving puzzles. The English alphabet and its corresponding Ardois pattern are shown below. Use this chart to decipher the code about famous ships.

A	● ○
B	○ ● ● ●
C	○ ● ○ ●
D	○ ● ●
E	●
F	● ● ○ ●
G	○ ○ ●
H	● ● ● ●
I	● ●
J	● ○ ○ ○
K	○ ● ○
L	● ○ ● ●
M	○ ○
N	○ ●
O	○ ○ ○
P	● ○ ○ ●
Q	○ ○ ● ○
R	● ○ ●
S	● ● ●
T	○
U	● ● ○
V	● ● ● ○
W	● ○ ○
X	○ ● ● ○
Y	○ ● ○ ○
Z	○ ○ ● ●

ARDOIS

The following terms or phrases associated with famous ships are in a message for you to decipher. Use the deciphered code clue to identify the vessel. Jot down your answers for both the code and the ship "between the lines" and then turn the page to check them.

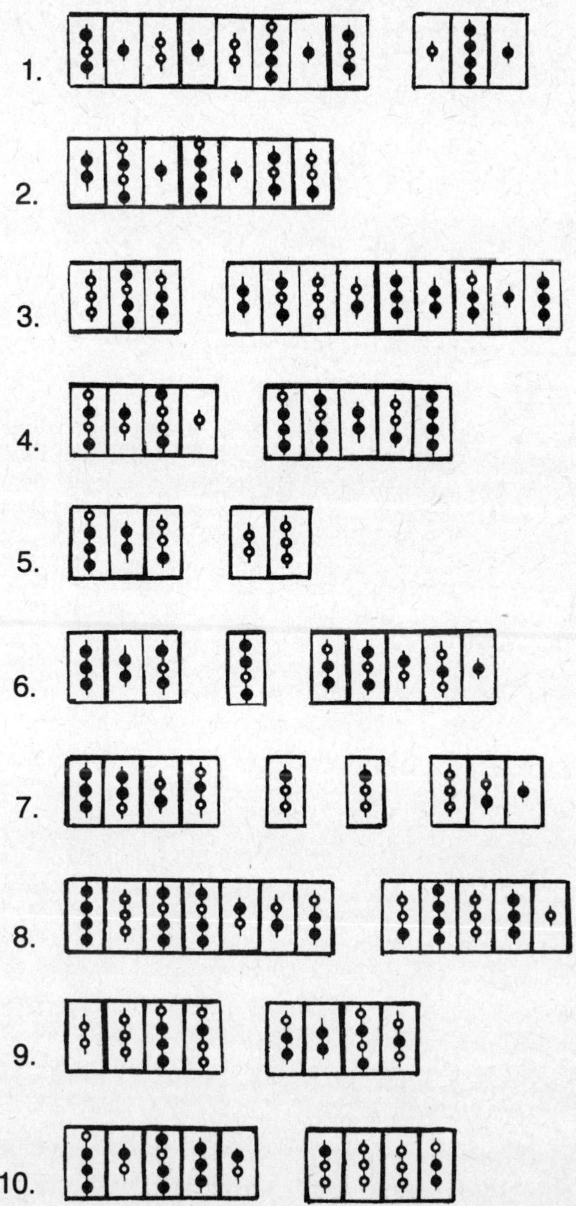

1.

2.

3.

4.

5.

6.

7.

8.

9.

10.

ARDOIS
answers

	CODE	SHIP
1.	Remember the	*Maine*
2.	Iceberg	*Titanic*
3.	Old Ironsides	*Constitution*
4.	Capt. Bligh	*Bounty*
5.	Big Mo	*Missouri*
6.	Sir F. Drake	*Golden Hind*
7.	Sunk W.W. One	*Lusitania*
8.	Holland Ghost	*Flying Dutchman*
9.	Moby Dick	*Pequod*
10.	Balsa Wood	*Kon-Tiki*

ART

Whether varnishing woodwork or admiring a statue, many of us have daydreamed of being a palette pro. We've also looked at so-called masterpieces and said, "I can do that!" Before raising your brushes, put on your brain beret and master these.

1. This woman's "portrait in black and gray" was completed by her son. Some say he did so by whistling the hours away. Who was she?

2. He painted a "cheerful" lady while he pondered birds' means of flight.

3. This lady needed more than a hand when she was rescued from the island of Melos.

4. Which American sculptor is credited with creating the lightweight, colorful art of mobiles?

5. What Oriental art style creates unique figures from paper?

6. What painting style makes use of light and shaded areas to achieve a third dimension on canvas?

7. This Swiss intellectual movement called for a return to innocence as well as odd symbolism in the arts.

8. Which type of painting uses only gray tints to give the effect of sculpture in relief?

9. What art form was created by French Impressionists who used pinlike points of color?

10. Paper artists use this German word for scissor cutting to describe their special designs.

ART

answers

1. Of course, she was the mother of James Abbott McNeill Whistler.

2. Leonardo da Vinci. La Gioconda (*Mona Lisa*) was the lady with the enigmatic smile.

3. The *Venus de Milo*. This marble statue of Venus with no arms became a sensation in 1820 when it was discovered on the island of Melos, one of the Cyclades in the Aegean.

4. Alexander Calder.

5. Origami (Japanese: "paper folding").

6. Chiaroscuro (Italian: clear dark). Photographers also use light and shadow for similar effects.

7. The Dada movement. The term was picked by Tristan Tsara, the group's leader, because of its meaninglessness. Dadaists flourished in Europe from 1916 to 1922. Their style created fantastic symbolic expressions in the arts.

8. Grisaille (French: *gris*, gray).

9. Pointillism. In this style, a white canvas or base is systematically covered with small points of pure color. When viewed from a distance, these same points seem to blend together to give a luminous appearance to the viewer.

10. Scherenschnitte. Yes, it's as difficult to learn as it is to pronounce. However, once you've mastered it—wow!

ASTROLOGY

Even doubters have been known to take a peek at the newspaper horoscope for information about their birth sign. It's only human. In fact, it just may be more than human. It may very well be . . . Anyway, see what your lucky stars tell you about the questions below.

1. How many degrees are in each sign of the zodiac?
2. What is the one object sign among the zodiac's twelve?
3. Who are the twins of Gemini?
4. What is astrology's New Year's Day?
5. Can you name the three earth signs?
6. What does the word *zodiac* mean?
7. Who are the Dioscuri?
8. What do Aries, Leo, and Sagittarius have in common?
9. Why would an astrology student need an ephemeris?
10. What does an astrologer locate with an aspect finder?

ASTROLOGY

answers

1. Thirty degrees (30 × 12 zodiac houses = 360 degrees in the horoscope circle).

2. Libra, the Scales. It is the seventh sign and it is entered by the sun at the autumnal equinox. There are four human and seven animal houses.

3. Castor and Pollux, twin sons of Zeus, king of the gods in Greek mythology. Zeus made them immortal by placing them among the stars.

4. March 21, the vernal equinox.

5. Taurus, Virgo, and Capricorn. The "earth" in this case is one of the four main elements into which the sages of old divided all physical matter. The others are air, fire, and water.

6. Ring of animals. Obviously, this isn't completely accurate, for there are the human signs and Libra too.

7. Another name for Castor and Pollux.

8. They are the fire signs. (See answer 5 above.)

9. An ephemeris is a table that gives the computed location of a heavenly body during every day in a given period.

10. The configuration of the planets *and* stars as they relate to each other and to the astrologer.

BEAT THE STOPWATCH

Remember those popular radio and TV game shows in which the competitors had to race the minutes to make their choices? If you don't have a stopwatch, you can use a clock with a second hand. Pit yourself against time as you answer. Ready, set, go!

1. According to legend, how many Wise Men were there?
2. Pro basketball awards this number of points for a difficult shot.
3. How many points are in a football field goal?
4. How many angles are in an isosceles triangle?
5. The Chicago Cubs had a famous infield combination. How many players were named in this particular group?
6. How many Brontë sisters were there?
7. What is the number of poems in a tetralogy?
8. What is the square root of 9?
9. In the song, how many coins were in the fountain?
10. What was the number of witches who foretold Macbeth's fate?

BEAT THE STOPWATCH

answers

1. Three.
2. Three.
3. Three.
4. Three.
5. Three (Tinkers to Evers to Chance).
6. Three (Charlotte, Emily, and Anne).
7. Four (Greek: *tetra*, four + *logos*, word).
8. Three.
9. Three ("Three Coins in the Fountain").
10. Three.

BIBLE

The massive collection of faith and fact in the Bible is an invaluable treasure for trivia fans. From Genesis to Revelations, here are some of the most unusual.

1. In what town did Jesus learn his trade of carpentry?
2. One of many Bible saints, he is the first listed in major dictionaries.
3. If you disobey the Decalogue's rules, what laws have you broken?
4. She saved the Jewish nation and caused an evil executioner to perish by his own device.
5. Legend has it that this disciple, an artist and a physician, created a portrait of the Virgin Mary.
6. We all know about Cain and Abel. But who was Adam and Eve's third son?
7. Speaking of threes, what do these three names have in common: Ararat, Sinai, and Pisgah?
8. From what modern-day region did the Queen of Sheba, who charmed King Solomon, actually come?
9. For Methuselah to have lived so long, he must have had unusual parents. Can you name his father?
10. Along with Joshua, he was the only other man permitted to enter the Promised Land of Canaan after it was sighted by the Wandering Tribes.

BIBLE

answers

1. Nazareth.

2. Aaron. He was the older brother of Moses and the high priest of the Hebrews.

3. The Ten Commandments. Decalogue, another name for them, is derived from Latin and French.

4. Esther. Haman, a Persian official, sought to destroy the Jews. However, Esther exposed his schemes to the Persian king, Ahasuerus (Xerxes). Haman was then executed by his own device, the hangman's noose.

5. Luke. In Colossians 4:14, he is called the "beloved physician." Many Bible scholars also believe that he was a Gentile and thus the only Gentile biblicist.

6. Seth. In Genesis 4:25, he is described as being born soon after Cain killed Abel.

7. Ararat: the series of hills upon which Noah's Ark reputedly came to rest. Sinai: the mount from which Moses descended with the Ten Commandments. Pisgah: the heights from which Moses was permitted to see the Promised Land.

8. Southern Arabia. Sheba was the biblical name for Saba, an ancient kingdom in the southern Arabian peninsula.

9. Enoch. A brief story of his life is told in Genesis 5:18–24.

10. Caleb. He and Joshua were the only two of the twelve spies sent into Canaan who encouraged the Hebrews to enter. Because of their truthful and righteous ways, they alone were permitted permanent entrance.

BLACK HISTORY

The accomplishments of black Americans are detailed throughout this book. Here is a compilation of varied achievements.

1. What do Tom Bradley, Coleman Young, and Harold Washington have in common?
2. She won three gold medals in track and field in the 1960 Olympics.
3. Who was called the "Black Moses" for her efforts to free slaves?
4. Who won the Nobel peace prize and was instrumental in several Middle Eastern negotiations?
5. She was the first black Congresswoman from Texas.
6. The "honest" name of this former slave gave hope to many.
7. His writing makes him a poet laureate in anyone's book.
8. Which musician composed the theme song of Harry Truman's successful 1948 campaign?
9. What was the distinction of the Alpha Kappa Alpha sorority?
10. This rodeo star is correctly credited with inventing the bulldogging competition.

BLACK HISTORY

answers

1. They are the mayors of Los Angeles, Detroit, and Chicago respectively.

2. Wilma Rudolph. She left the Russian "amateurs" with their shoestrings dragging.

3. Harriet Tubman.

4. Ralph Bunche. An educator and statesman, he received the Nobel prize in 1950.

5. Barbara Jordan.

6. Sojourner Truth. Freed by New York's state emancipation laws, she worked diligently for abolition.

7. Langston Hughes.

8. Eubie Blake. He wrote "I'm Just Wild About Harry" and many other popular songs.

9. It was the first sorority at Howard University in Washington, D.C.

10. Bill Pickett.

BLACK HISTORY II

The record of black achievement continues.

1. He was the first black American ambassador to the UN.
2. As a Supreme Court justice since the 1960s, this man has been involved in many crucial decisions.
3. What did Emmett Ashford contribute to the sports world?
4. Who won an Oscar for her memorable performance in *Gone with the Wind*?
5. Which successful woman golfer also won at the Wimbledon tennis tournament in 1957?
6. He was an influential educator and author in early 1900s America.
7. A journalist, he was the director of the United States Information Agency (USIA) in the 1960s.
8. What did the Fighting 369th contribute to America's defense?
9. Can you name three of the main founders of the Congress of Racial Equality (CORE)?
10. This influential labor leader was instrumental in the negotiations with porters and the Pullman union.

BLACK HISTORY II

answers

1. Andrew Young.

2. Thurgood Marshall.

3. He was the first black umpire in the major leagues.

4. Hattie McDaniel.

5. Althea Gibson.

6. W. E. B. DuBois.

7. Carl Rowan.

8. They were an all-black unit in World War I. Their heroism was shown through some of the war's most difficult sieges.

9. Roy Wilkins, James Farmer, and Bayard Rustin.

10. A. Phillip Randolph.

BODY (HUMAN, THAT IS)

How well do you think you know yourself? Remember those general science classes that once seemed so useless? Don't you wish you'd *studied* more then? Aw shucks, no*body* but you is keeping score . . .

1. Which gland is called the master gland?
2. These tough tissues connect muscles to bones.
3. From this small, elongated form of protein, your race, age, and even your sex can be determined.
4. Why in the world would a surgeon be looking for McBirney's point?
5. Name the strange illness that would suddenly make you unable to understand this sentence or any of the ones above.
6. What is a Grecian profile?
7. Which human "islands" produce a substance necessary to counteract diabetes and other diseases?
8. What are camphoraceous, musky, floral, pepperminty, ethereal, pungent, and putrid?
9. What part of the body contains the pollux?
10. Can you name the body's "passage of emotion"?

BODY (HUMAN, THAT IS)

answers

1. The pituitary. This endocrine gland attached to a stalk at the brain's base affects growth and metabolism.

2. Tendons join muscles to bones.

3. A single strand of your hair.

4. This part of the body helps a surgeon locate the appendix on the large intestine.

5. Aphasia, a partial or total loss of the ability to use or understand words.

6. It is the description of a person whose forehead and nose form a straight line when seen in profile.

7. The islands, or islets, or Langerhans. Found in groups of cells in the pancreas, they produce the hormone insulin.

8. The major types of aromas or odors. Theoretically all scents are some combination of these.

9. Your hand. The pollux is your thumb.

10. Schlem's canal, better known as a tear duct.

BOTANY

From petals to roots, plants have always held a strange fascination—they are a world of their own. The following questions are but a microcosmic sampling of that special world.

1. With what basic plant function are pistils and stamens involved?
2. What are turpentine and pitch obtained from?
3. Can you name the source of cork?
4. Three of the edible members of this fungi are called oyster, puffball, and parasol. What does a pileus mean to them?
5. At what time of the year would you look for a Johnny-jump-up? By the way, what is it?
6. What parasitic apple tree growth is an osculator's favorite?
7. This tall grass, with droplike, grayish white seeds, is named after a biblical man who was often tormented for his faith.
8. What popular holiday shrub was a contribution of our first ambassador to Mexico?
9. Why is the word *peanut* a misnomer?
10. To what plant family do green donkey ears, silk pin cushions, cone heads, and fish hooks belong?

BOTANY

answers

1. Reproduction. The pistil is the seed-bearing organ; the stamen is the pollen-bearing organ.

2. Pines and other coniferous trees. Pitch is a resin and turpentine is an oleoresin.

3. Cork comes from the outer bark of certain Mediterranean oak trees, especially from Spain and Portugal.

4. They are varieties of mushroom. The pileus is a mushroom's cap.

5. It is an early spring violet.

6. The mistletoe.

7. Job's tears.

8. The poinsettia. In 1829, Ambassador Joel Poinsett brought this native South American shrub to the United States.

9. The peanut is a vine of the pea family with seed pods that ripen underground.

10. Cacti.

VISUAL QUIZ NUMBER TWO

BRAILLE

BRAILLE

Braille is a system of printing and writing for the blind. A series of raised dots distinguishes punctuation, numerals, and letters. Its inventor was Louis Braille, who was blind himself.

A	
B	
C	
D	
E	
F	
G	
H	
I	

J	
K	
L	
M	
N	
O	
P	
Q	
R	

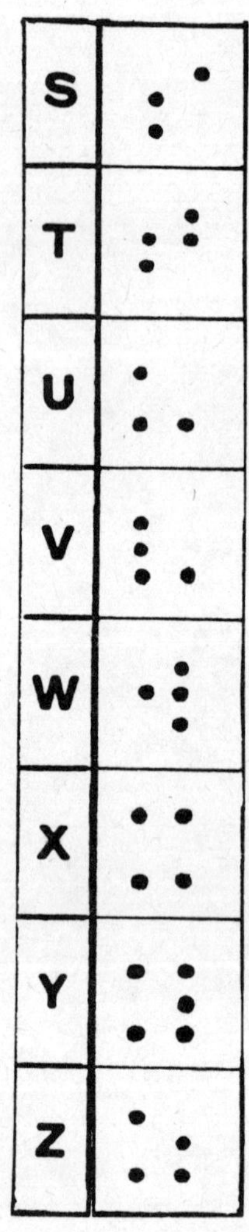

BRAILLE

Louis Braille accomplished much in spite of his sight loss. Apply his system below to learn about other courageous achievers and those who aided them. Jot down your answers for both the code and the achiever/aide "between the lines" and then turn the page to check them.

1.

2.

3.

4.

5.

6.

7.

8.

9.

10.

BRAILLE

answers

	CODE	ACHIEVER/AIDE
1.	Valiant lady	Helen Keller
2.	Lady's teacher	Ann Sullivan (She was Helen Keller's dedicated instructor and friend.)
3.	French artist	Toulouse-Lautrec (His art enabled this physically misshapen artist to achieve stature.)
4.	Deaf school	Thomas Hopkins Gallaudet (He founded America's first school for the deaf.)
5.	Little Stevie	Stevie Wonder (His music helps many see more clearly.)
6.	Deaf ninth	Beethoven (He wrote his Ninth Symphony when he was deaf.)
7.	Campobello	Franklin D. Roosevelt (He overcame polio.)
8.	Elephant man	John Merrick (His bravery has been depicted in movie, play, and book form.)
9.	Catcher	Roy Campanella (He survived an accident that left him paralyzed and inspires us today.)
10.	Polio ease	Nurse Elizabeth Kenny (Before Salk and Sabin, her treatments for polio helped many.)

CAPITAL REBUS

A rebus is a puzzle that consists of representations of objects, signs, or pictures. The sounds of their names suggest various words or phrases. Use these rebus puzzles to identify state capitals. Then name the particular capital's state. Jot down your answers for both the capital and the state "between the lines" and then turn the page to check them.

CAPITAL REBUS

answers

	CAPITAL	STATE
1.	Heart + ford (Harftord)	Connecticut
2.	Tree + ton (Trenton)	New Jersey
3.	Jack + sun (Jackson)	Mississippi
4.	Sail + lamb (Salem)	Oregon
5.	Lance + sing (Lansing)	Michigan
6.	Links + coins (Lincoln)	Nebraska
7.	Indian + apples + hiss (Indianapolis)	Indiana
8.	Hair + iceberg (Harrisburg)	Pennsylvania
9.	Baton + rouge (Baton Rouge)	Louisiana
10.	Buoys + see (Boise)	Idaho

CAPITAL REBUS II

Here's another round of captivating capital rebus puzzles! Jot down your answers for both the capital and the state "between the lines" and then turn the page to check them.

1. + Fee $

2. +

3. +

4. + A + + EEE!

5. Want + +

6. (Abbrev.) + +

7. Oh! + + E + AH!

8. + +

9. + + +

10. + + A

CAPITAL REBUS II

answers

	CAPITAL	STATE
1.	Santa + fee (Santa Fe)	New Mexico
2.	Frank + fort (Frankfort)	Kentucky
3.	Spring + field (Springfield)	Illinois
4.	Tail + a + horse + EEE (Tallahassee)	Florida
5.	Ad + land + tee (Atlanta)	Georgia
6.	Mountain (Mt.) + peel + ear (Montpelier)	Vermont
7.	Oh! + leap + E + ah! (Olympia)	Washington
8.	Tall + band + knee (Albany)	New York
9.	Sack + cry + man + toe (Sacramento)	California
10.	Hell + lean + a (Helena)	Montana

CAPITAL REBUS (WORLD)

This time take a global guess—or better yet use these rebus clues to link world capitals to their respective countries. Jot down your answers for both the capital and the nation "between the lines" and then turn the page to check them.

1. +

2. + + Oh!

3. + L's

4. + WAAA!

5. + Going Going

6. CAW! + +

7. TIN + Candy + A

8. +

9. + + A +

10. Want + + A + BAA!

CAPITAL REBUS (WORLD)

answers

	CAPITAL	NATION
1.	Pear + wrist (Paris)	France
2.	Toe + key + oh! (Tokyo)	Japan
3.	Brush + I's (Brussels)	Belgium
4.	Anchor + waaa! (Ankara)	Turkey
5.	Rain + gone (Rangoon)	Burma
6.	Caw! + eye + row (Cairo)	Egypt
7.	Can + bar + a (Canberra)	Australia
8.	Car + bull (Kabul)	Afghanistan
9.	Sun + tea + a + goat (Santiago)	Chile
10.	Ad + Dot (Addis) Abe + a + baa! (Ababa)	Ethiopia

CARTOONS

Ah, remember watching Saturday morning cartoons while munching a big bowl of cornflakes? Now don't forget your orange juice as you test your memory here.

1. Who were George and his futuristic family?
2. This George had friends who belonged in a zoo.
3. She was queen of her tropical domain.
4. His dog was named Mighty Manfred.
5. He often fought Oilcan Harry to save Pearl Pureheart.
6. This sidekick of Huckleberry Hound liked to sing "My Darling, Clementine."
7. Can you name Woody Woodpecker's niece and nephew?
8. She was Dudley Dooright's endangered girlfriend.
9. His dog, Mr. Peabody, invented the Way Back Machine.
10. This adventure series featured the most realistic lips in all cartoondom.

CARTOONS

answers

1. *The Jetsons*.

2. George of the Jungle.

3. Sheena, Queen of the Jungle.

4. Tom Terrific.

5. Mighty Mouse. Oh, the thrill of it when he flew into action!

6. Augie Doggie.

7. Knothead (niece), Splinter (nephew).

8. Nell. She was constantly tormented by the dastardly Snidely Whiplash.

9. He was Sherman, a bright young man in his own way.

10. *Clutch Cargo.* This series had the unique feature of using an actual person's lips to do the speaking for the character.

CHILDREN'S LITERATURE

Evil witches, princesses, warlocks, heroes, and adventurers may be found on the wonderfully thrilling pages of children's books. Here is but a sample.

1. A jealous queen tried to ruin the good medical advice, "An apple a day keeps the doctor away." In what story did this green-eyed ruler try her tricks?

2. Briar Rose and Malificent are associated with a much better-known title. What is it?

3. What popular heroine's mystery-adventure series did Carolyn Keane write?

4. Where were Chimneyville, Torpedo Town, and the Blue Forest located?

5. Why did Beauty agree to marry the horrible Beast?

6. Who was Beatrix Potter's mischievous "hare-raiser"?

7. Near what well-known body of land did the ship *Hispaniola* anchor?

8. Who was the Griffin's weeping friend in Wonderland?

9. Which foxy fellow persuaded Pinocchio to leave school?

10. Why doesn't never-never land exist, even in James Barrie's *Peter Pan*?

CHILDREN'S LITERATURE
answers

1. *Snow White.*
2. *Sleeping Beauty.*
3. Nancy Drew.
4. Oz. The Emerald City was Dorothy's destination.
5. To save her father's life.
6. Peter Rabbit. (Flopsy, Mopsy, and Cottontail were siblings.)
7. It was near Treasure Island, also the title of Stevenson's novel.
8. The Mock Turtle.
9. The fox, J. Worthington Fowlfellow.
10. Peter Pan's fantasy land was named Neverland. Thus, never-never land did not exist in the story.

CHINA

Once a forbidden land to most Westerners, China and the West are again developing good diplomatic relations. As that progress continues, good luck with these questions.

1. This is the one man-made structure that can be discerned on earth from outer space.

2. They called themselves the "righteous uniting band" but were mistakently called "uniting fists" during their rebellion against foreigners in 1900.

3. What was the special name for the diplomacy that helped restore Sino-U.S. relations in the early 1970s?

4. Can you name the European adventurer who served as the mayor of Yang-chau for three years?

5. One of China's earliest religions was Taoism. Who was its founder?

6. We've all heard about Confucius. Can you name his collection of teachings?

7. What caused Marco Polo to believe that Kublai Khan had discovered an alchemist's secret for special money?

8. How did a river's castoffs make the former Chinese port of Chinkiang an inland city?

9. How did a young woman from Salem, Massachusetts, change an entire city's trade policy?

10. Who were the geomancers of old Cathay and how did they influence Chinese architecture and city planning for centuries to come?

CHINA

answers

1. China's Great Wall. It is 2,500 miles long and stretches across more than one twentieth of the circumference of the earth.

2. They were called the Boxers (Chinese: *I-He-Chuan*, righteous uniting band). Their unsuccessful revolt led to harsh economics and territorial concession payments to colonial powers.

3. Ping-pong diplomacy. The term derives from U.S. and Chinese exchanges of table tennis teams as well as from Henry Kissinger's secret missions.

4. Marco Polo. He was in China from 1271 to 1295 and was granted this chance by Kublai Khan.

5. The philosopher Lao-Tse.

6. They were the Analects. Confucius, also known as Kung Fu-tse, taught devotion to family and friends as well as ancestor worship.

7. The Chinese were using paper money, which was unheard of in Europe at that time.

8. Over many years, the Yangtze River has left so much silt that Chinkiang's location has been changed by 150 miles.

9. Before 1834, Canton was China's only port of entry for foreigners (and admitted only men). A young American woman, disguised as a boy, was caught in a trading office. This "incident" caused a temporary break in China-U.S. trade. Fortunately, she and the trade survived.

10. The geomancers (Chinese: earth diviners) were similar to astrologers. They placed metal disks inscribed with astronomy signs on magnetic stones. From the various sign positions, they read "lines of force" across the land. Entire towns were built around centers of energy concentration or dispersal.

CLOTHES

We admire or envy clothes on others, strain our diets to fit into them, and must wear at least a minimum amount of clothes or risk shocking prune-faced grumpies. Anyway, why not try these on for size?

1. This type of silk tie is named after the ruling family of England since 1917.
2. The girl who "couldn't stop dancing" was wearing a pair of these.
3. This soft woolen material comes from a species of goat.
4. If a mukluk isn't a fashion critic, what is it?
5. What is the most logical place to wear a Korean fly cage?
6. What do Nimes (France) and Dunga (India) have in common with Levi Strauss?
7. How is the body's longest muscle associated with clothing (men's especially) and tailoring?
8. What does a Moslem expounder of religious law have in common with a type of casual clothes?
9. In the Moslem culture, what is a yashmak? *Clue:* Its use heightens the desire for its disuse.
10. What are broguings?

CLOTHES

answers

1. A Windsor, cut on the bias and tied in a double bow.

2. *Red Shoes*, says Hans Christian Andersen, author of the well-known story.

3. Cashmere. The goats are from Kashmir and Tibet.

4. A shoe worn by Eskimos.

5. On your head. It is a hat.

6. In general, blue jeans. Nimes is credited as the originating point for denim, or serge, a twilled cotton cloth. Dunga was the source point of dungrı, a coarse cotton cloth. The word eventually became dungarees.

7. The muscle is the sartorius, located in the thigh. Sartorial, referring to tailoring, derives from the tailor's crossed legs. The sartorius makes this possible by allowing the leg to rotate.

8. They are both called mufti. To military personnel, mufti are civilian clothes.

9. A woman's double veil worn in public.

10. The decorative perforation in heavy oxford shoes (Irish: *brōg,* shoe). It also is seen in wing-tipped shoes.

COMICS (IN PRINT)

No matter how bad the news may be, we can always lose ourselves in the humor and adventure of the comics. Recall the thrills and laughter as you give your answers.

1. This web-footed cutie is Donald Duck's girlfriend.

2. Can you give the full name of Popeye's hamburger-munching friend?

3. LuAnn, Margo, Tommy, and others lived in this always busy apartment.

4. Name Broomhilda's best buzzard and troll friends.

5. To the Green Hornet, who were Kato and Black Beauty?

6. Who became Captain Marvel by saying what magic word?

7. Introduced in 1955, he is the adorable orphan of the comics.

8. What did Wiley and Thor do in prehistoric times?

9. He is "the ghost who walks." Can you name his girlfriend and pet wolf?

10. Bitten by a radiation-polluted spider, he became Spider Man. Name him.

COMICS (IN PRINT)

answers

1. Daisy.
2. J. Wellington Wimpy.
3. "Apartment 3-G."
4. Gaylord the Buzzard and Irwin the Troll.
5. His sidekick and his car respectively.
6. Billy Batson. He said, "Shazam!"
7. Dondi.
8. In "B.C.," Wiley is the one-legged poet and Thor is an inventor.
9. The Phantom. His lady is Diana and his wolf is Devil.
10. Peter Parker, the ol' web-slinger.

CURIOSITIES

Whether in Ripley's *Believe It or Not* or in our own attics, we can often find the unusual and the bizarre. Sometimes on a rainy day, we even hope we will—right? Now get cozy in that easy chair and see if you can categorize these curiosities.

1. Who was the American chimp who orbited twice in 1961? *Clue*: His name is the same as the young cop of *Hazzard County*.

2. What is a horse called if it has not yet won a race?

3. This form of Oriental self-defense actually means "gentle struggle" or "soft art."

4. The pronunciation of this herb of the mint family suggests a watch. What is it?

5. They have drums but no band, shoes but no feet.

6. Many men wanted to waltz with the woman whose name is Australian slang for a backpack. Who was she?

7. This Greek poet's name is the same as a current-day electrically charged particle.

8. What do a short piano composition, a trifle, and a billiards-like game have in common?

9. What is a Job's comforter?

10. If you suffer from the malady known as Devil's pinches, why should you not play even a touch football game?

CURIOSITIES

answers

1. Enos.

2. Maiden. This is true for male and female horses.

3. Jujitsu (Japanese: *ju*, soft or pliant + *jutsu*, art). In this Japanese system, leverage and the adversary's own strength are used against him.

4. Thyme (pronounced "time"). This plant has white, pink, or red flowers and fragrant leaves that are used for food seasoning.

5. The brakes of an auto.

6. Matilda.

7. Ion.

8. Each is a bagatelle. The billiards version is played with nine balls on a table with nine holes.

9. A person who actually aggravates one's misery while pretending to comfort.

10. You bruise easily and badly.

DINING

From soup to nuts, here is a menu filled with mental entrées for your enjoyment.

1. This flavoring, one of America's favorites, comes from the black beans of a climbing orchid.
2. Some of its names are globe and Jerusalem and its heart is a delicacy.
3. What is the source of the delicacy chitlins?
4. In French, it means "to chop." In the U.S., it is often "slinged" alongside Adam and Eve on a raft.
5. This succulent fungus is snootily sniffed out by pigs.
6. They are called "the speedy ones," but a good fork master can beat them any day.
7. What is the German name for beef or pork that is marinated in vinegar before cooking?
8. This alga is a Japanese wedding feast favorite since it symbolizes prosperity and longevity.
9. On the menu of what country in particular would you find a haggis?
10. Which mild salad dressing was hastily created by a man who ordinarily dined in the nude?

DINING

answers

1. Vanilla.

2. An artichoke.

3. Chitlins (also called chitterlings) are a pig's small intestines.

4. Good ol' hash (chopped meat and sometimes vegetables), often served with eggs on toast.

5. Truffles (Latin: *tuber*, a knob or swelling). These are fleshy, edible, potato-shaped fungi grown underground.

6. Chopsticks (Pidgin English for Chinese: *k'wai-tsze,* the quick ones).

7. Sauerbraten.

8. Seaweed.

9. On many menus in Scotland. It is a predominantly Scottish dish made of the lungs, heart, and other organs of a sheep or calf. It is mixed with suet, seasonings, and oatmeal.

10. Mayonnaise. It was reputedly created by the Duke de la Richelieu, who often brunched in the buff. He was in Mahon, Minorca. There he rapidly attired himself and a hastily prepared salad for a surprise visit from Napoleon. He "garbed" the vegetables with egg yolks, olive oil, and vinegar.

DRINKS

From Tequila sunrises to bedtime toddies, here's a toast to all concoctions past and present. Skoal and mud in your eye!

1. What is either the second game of a baseball doubleheader or a wee-hours drink?
2. This word sounds like a cad found in a singles' bar and also describes certain wines.
3. Can you name a "sling's" famous Asian port and its two main ingredients?
4. Which word for a tall, mixed drink is also a railroad term for proceed?
5. What do a 1½-ounce drink measure and a billiards cue support have in common?
6. How are an old British naval surgeon and a carpenter's tool related to a modern drink?
7. Where did the childhood expression "Mind your P's and Q's" originate?
8. What do Badoit, Fachigen, and Ramlösa have in common?
9. Why is the word *whisky* in Irish whisky wrong?
10. When did John Styth Pemberton take "the pause that refreshes"?

DRINKS
answers

1. Nightcap.

2. Brut.

3. Singapore. Gin and brandy.

4. Highball. The railroad term derived from a signal system in which a large circular sign was raised as a sign to proceed. Some engineers literally speeded up—thus the connection to speed.

5. Both are a jigger. The billiards cue support is also called a bridge.

6. Both are named gimlet, as is the beverage. The British naval surgeon began serving lime juice with gin to prevent scurvy among sailors. The tool is a boring device with a handle, shaft, and spiral cutting edge.

7. In English pubs, patrons' orders were compiled on a board marked *P* and *Q*, indicating pints and quarts.

8. All are European mineral waters—from France, West Germany, and Sweden, respectively.

9. Irish rye and bourbon are correctly spelled *whiskey*. Canadian and Scotch brands are spelled *whisky*.

10. A pharmacist in Atlanta, Georgia, he developed the original Coca-Cola formula in 1886.

EARTH

Earth is our mother planet, the "big blue marble," and to some the object of much UFO interest. See what you know about our planetary member of the universe.

1. Where did the geocentric theory of the universe place the earth?
2. Which theory changed the geocentric view and shocked the world?
3. Can you name the three main levels from the earth's inner core to the surface?
4. Who were the Roman and the Greek goddesses who personified the earth?
5. Who supposedly boasted that he could move the earth if he could just find a place to stand?
6. What is the tectonic plate theory? According to its suppositions, which two great continents might once have been joined?
7. Do you know the lowest point on the earth's surface? The deepest point of all?
8. What two geographical places are closest to the earth's center?
9. Neither the Sahara nor the Gobi is the driest place on earth. Do you know the only desert in which rain has never been seen?
10. What is *morketiden* and why is it of special concern in Tromso, Norway?

EARTH

answers

1. At the center of what was thought to be the universe.

2. The heliocentric theory, proposed by the Polish astronomer Nicolaus Copernicus. The idea that the planets might revolve around the sun shocked many scientists and religious zealots alike.

3. The three main levels are the magma (molten core), the mantle, and the crust.

4. Tellus (Roman) and Gaea (Greek).

5. The Greek mathematician and physicist Archimedes. He needed a place to stand to apply his principles of the lever.

6. A theory involving the shifting movements of the earth's crust. Some tectonic theorists believe Africa and South America may once have been connected.

7. The lowest surface point is the Dead Sea. The deepest-known point is the Marianas Trench in the Pacific.

8. At the poles. The earth is flatter there because of its rotation. In fact, the poles are ten miles closer to the earth's center than is the equator.

9. At an extremely arid site called Calama in the Atacama Desert in Chile.

10. Tromso, Norway, is the world's northernmost city. *Morketiden*, the Arctic darkness, naturally lasts longest there.

ENGLISH EQUIVALENTS

Have you ever watched one of those well-made British films but had a bit o'trouble with their terminology? Here are some examples for your edification. Can you "translate" them?

1. Windcheater
2. Nappy
3. Lift
4. Trunk call
5. Pram
6. Draper
7. Draughts
8. Bespoke
9. Paraffin
10. Pantechnicon

ENGLISH EQUIVALENTS
answers

1. Windbreaker
2. Diaper
3. Elevator
4. Long-distance call
5. Baby carriage
6. Dry goods store
7. Checkers
8. Custom made
9. Kerosene
10. Moving van

FADS

From the Charleston to Superball, fads have captured the imagination of America and often of the world. Here is a collection of the truly trendy.

1. What frontier hero's story was the basis for the coonskin cap craze?

2. Within four years of the cap craze above, which fad was sweeping and swirling across the United States with a Hawaiian accent?

3. This hairstyle was popularized by a 10.

4. The twist whirled around in the early 1960s. Do you know the particular mint and the lounge associated with it?

5. In the 1930s, hot shots tied certain mammals' appendages to their car antennas. Can you name these unusual "ornaments"?

6. This box with a money-grabbing hand had the same name as a chilling 1951 movie about an outerspace visitor. What were they both called?

7. What squeezy object could pick up newsprint and came in an egg-shaped container?

8. In the 1920s this portable answer to a speakeasy made some rumble seats even more bumpy.

9. These cylindrical objects, commonly thought of as toys, began their existence as weapons in the Pacific.

10. In the 1940s, Shipwreck Kelly was just one of a number of people who gained fame by sitting in a rather odd place. What was it?

FADS

answers

1. Davy Crockett.

2. Hula hoops.

3. Cornrows as worn by Bo Derek in the movie *10*.

4. The mint was peppermint and the Peppermint Lounge (in New York) was the place. There Hank Ballard is credited by many with beginning the "twist" music that gained wider popularity wih Chubby Checker.

5. They were squirrels' tails. These hot shots were "furry" indeed, as many sported raccoon coats as well.

6. The Thing. The box contained a clutching hand that grasped coins placed on its top. The movie of the same name involved an Arctic research team that battled a powerful, manlike creature from another world.

7. Silly Putty.

8. The hip flask. After some bumpy rides, this many-shaped container ended up being placed inside coat pockets.

9. They are yo-yos.

10. He was considered by "experts" to be America's champion flagpole sitter. Though a real oddity, this fad required full reserves of both courage and stamina.

FASHIONS

Here is another collection of clothes trivia. Somewhere between the outlandish and the practical you will find the "pattern" involved.

1. Named after a Scottish clan, these sweaters and socks have a diamond-shaped pattern that often comes in two colors.
2. What early variation of Narragansett Indian footwear affected everything from hunting to warfare?
3. To what durable item of fashion did Genoa, Italy, contribute?
4. What modern-day skirt lowered the eyebrows of the public while raising the brows of its designers?
5. How did the "Grecian bend" throw a curve into the clothing industry?
6. What patriotic unifier of Italy's provinces contributed his name to a woman's loose-fitting blouse?
7. What pre-World War I skirt made sitting easier than walking and falling the easiest of all?
8. Can you name three articles of clothing that were uniquely linked because of a controversial war?
9. What do a sofa, an overcoat, and a cigarette have in common with a stylish English peerage?
10. Can you identify the headgear that received its name from a well-known poem?

FASHIONS

answers

1. Argyle. Argyll is a county on the west coast of Scotland.

2. The moccasin. From the Narragansett word *mokussin,* this heelless, soft leather footgear aided the Indians in stalking both game and enemies, especially bright-garbed, heavy-booted soldiers.

3. Jeans. The word is an Anglicized version of Genoa, where the particular cloth was made. Other cities and cloths added to the style too.

4. The midi. The style was created as a change from the popular mini. However, its designers' brows arched swiftly as their profits fell sharply.

5. In the late eighteenth century, women had to bend forward when they walked because of their confining corsets and bustles. This style was called Grecian, though possible connections with Greek fashion or art are obscure.

6. Giuseppe Garibaldi who unified Italy with the help of Guiseppe Mazzini. Their followers were noted for wearing loose shirts with full sleeves. With an added high collar, this became the women's blouse style known as the garibaldi.

7. The hobble skirt. From 1910 to 1914 this long skirt came in so narrow below the knees that it hindered the wearer's basic movements.

8. The Balaclava helmet, the Cardigan sweater, and the Raglan overcoat all originated during the Crimean War (1854–1856). The British had a major base at Balaclava (Balaklava). The Earl of Cardigan was an officer in the ill-fated Light Brigade. Lord Raglan was the overall British commander.

9. Britain's Chesterfield family gave its title to all three.

10. The tam-o'-shanter. It is named after the hero of Robert Burns's poem *Tam o'Shanter*.

FIRSTS

Are you wondering why this segment wasn't first? Only because the word *first* does not begin with an *A*. Who can argue with the alphabet?

1. Who was Chicago's first female mayor?

2. Who was the first Pope to visit England?

3. Mr. and Mrs. Brown of Bristol, England, became famous in 1978 for a natural event that happened in a most unusual way. What was it?

4. On June 24, 1947, an Air Force pilot first noticed one of these near Mt. Ranier, Washington.

5. Who was the first actress to win an Oscar?

6. Speaking of movies, what was the first movie to have a series of sequels?

7. Who was the first honorary citizen of the United States?

8. On July 12, 1933, the first minimum wage law became a reality in the United States. Would it buy you a cup of coffee today?

9. Abraham Lincoln was not the Republican party's first presidential candidate. Do you know who was?

10. She was America's very first congresswoman. Can you name her and the state which she proudly represented?

FIRSTS

answers

1. Jane Byrne held this distinct office.

2. Pope John Paul II.

3. They are the parents of the world's first test tube baby, Louise Brown, born July 25, 1978.

4. A UFO. These objects have been spotted often since then, especially during the month of September in the United States. Are they Pentagon secrets, Russian spies, or unemployed pie tin salespeople? Perhaps the Shadow kno-o-ows.

5. Janet Gaynor achieved this honor. The movie was *Seventh Heaven* made in 1927.

6. *The Thin Man* (1933). The sequels were *After the Thin Man* (1937), *Another Thin Man* (1938), *Shadow of the Thin Man* (1942), *The Thin Man Goes Home* (1944), *Song of the Thin Man* (1946).

7. The Marquis de Lafayette. This gallant Frenchman certainly earned his title for his crucial service in aiding America's Revolutionary War efforts.

8. No, it wouldn't, unless the coffee was at least two days old. However, the $.40-an-hour wage guarantee was very important in those depressed times.

9. John C. Fremont. An explorer and military hero, he embodied much of the frontier spirit that motivated Republican party members.

10. Jeannette Rankin was the lady and she quite capably represented Montana in the House of Representatives. She served during the years 1917–1919 and 1941–1943.

FOOD (FOR THOUGHT OR WHATEVER)

Here are more gustatory goodies to please your palate for trivia treats!

1. What do a small beefsteak cut from the loin tip and an association of people have in common?
2. This dried fruit of a seedless Mediterranean grape sounds very much like anything now in progress.
3. This pie, once made of the lesser parts of a deer, is now eaten by an apologetic person.
4. It can be a dandy's cologne, a jelly of meat, or tomato juice used as a relish.
5. What is curious about a pandowdy besides its name?
6. Can you define the difference between chop suey and chow mein?
7. In which place setting would you find a runcible spoon?
8. When serving à la Newburgh, what have you done?
9. What do chapati and puri have in common?
10. Can you describe a zabaglione?

FOOD (FOR THOUGHT OR WHATEVER)

answers

1. They are both a club.

2. Currant (current).

3. Humble pie. It might also be filled with an assortment of ill-advised words.

4. Aspic. It is a type of lavender, a relish, and also a seafood mold.

5. It is a deep-dish pudding or an apple pie that has only a top crust.

6. Chop suey (Chinese: *tsa-sui*, various pieces) consists of meat, bean sprouts, celery, and mushrooms and is served with *rice*. Chow mein (Chinese: *ch'ao*, to fry + *mein*, flour) consists of a stew of meat, onions, celery, and bean sprouts and is served with *fried noodles*.

7. It is found in the setting of Edward Lear's *The Owl and the Pussycat*. Furthermore, it isn't a spoon at all. Rather, it is a fork with two broad prongs and one sharp-edged, curved prong.

8. You've served in a style popular in Newburgh, Scotland. It is a sauce that consists of creamed egg yolks, wine, and butter.

9. They are breads of India. Chapati is a flat style, and puri has a puffy texture.

10. Zabaglione is an Italian confection of eggs, sugar, and fruit juice or wine that is beaten to thickness and served in a glass.

GAMES

As a participant or a fan, you probably find games to be everything from captivating to exasperating. May lady luck smile on you—and remember, it's only a . . .

1. In chess, these eight pieces are the same for either player.
2. What are a pair plus three of a kind called in poker?
3. On an American roulette wheel, what color are zero and double zero?
4. What would you be doing if you were in double dutch with the red hot peppers?
5. This game was played in Roman army camps in 100 B.C. *Clue*: "Leaners."
6. Created during the Depression by an architect, this game was first played with blueprint paper and wood. *Clue:* Its original names were Criss-Cross Words and Lexico.
7. Which card game uses a double deck of all cards above the 8 for 48 cards in all?
8. In which ring would you find the "inner bull," or "double bull"?
9. In a chuck-a-luck match, upon what do the gamblers bet?
10. "Hardway" and "shooter" are two terms from what game?

GAMES
answers

1. Pawns.

2. A full house.

3. They are both green.

4. Jumping rope. Double-dutch players use two ropes. Red hot peppers is a phrase used in jump-rope rhymes.

5. Horseshoes. A ringer is worth three points.

6. Scrabble.

7. Pinochle. It is similar to the French game of bezique. If you have the queen of spades and the jack of diamonds, you have pinochle!

8. In a dart board's innermost ring. It is worth 50 points to the dart player.

9. On the results of a three-dice throw.

10. Craps. It is a gambling game played with two dice. A first toss of seven or eleven wins. A beginning throw of two, three, or twelve loses.

    "Hardway" is the attempt to make an even numbered point by rolling the same number on two dice. Six the hardway is 3 + 3 instead of 4 + 2 or 5 + 1.

    "Shooter" is the person having his turn with the dice.

GAMES II

Hey, how many games do you know that have only one period, quarter, or round? Here's a chance to pick up some more points. Go for it!

1. What term refers to hitting a four-run homer in baseball or taking all the tricks in bridge?
2. This ecclesiastical member of the chess board moves diagonally.
3. A length of string is the only piece you need to play this "feline" game.
4. Which card game is a South American import that is similar to rummy?
5. What game uses the phrases "on the bar" and "lovers' leap"?
6. Similar to horseshoes, this competition also gives points for being close.
7. What game with pieces called "bams" and "cracks" was the rage in 1920s America?
8. What are the playing pieces in the game of ducks and drakes?
9. In which game would you find "squidges" and "grumps"?
10. Which competition calls for players to find rhymes for words that they give one another?

GAMES II

answers

1. A grand slam.

2. The bishop.

3. The children's game of cat's cradle.

4. Canasta. Meaning basket in Spanish, this game for two to six players uses a double deck and four jokers.

5. Backgammon.

6. Quoits. The object here is to score by tossing a ring of rope or flattened metal over a peg.

7. Mah-jong (Chinese: *ma-ch'iao*, house sparrow). This game is usually played by four persons. They use 136 to 144 domino-like tiles marked in suits and try to build combinations of them. Bams and craks are types of tiles.

8. Stones. In this game, the players try to skip stones the longest distance across a body of water.

9. Tiddlywinks. The players try to snap colored disks from a table or other surface into a cup by pressing the edges of the disks with larger disks. The terms squidges, grumps, and also squops are varied slang terms for the disks and the efforts to snap them.

10. Crambo (Latin: *crambe repetita*, cabbage repeatedly served).

GAMES III

This is it. Like being behind in the bottom of the ninth with two out, or having a minute to score from your own twenty-yard line, you've got one more chance to come out ahead in this category. Are you GAME?

1. If you're matching rooms, possible weapons, and suspects, which board game are you playing?

2. Which king is the one shown in profile on playing cards?

3. When would you use the Nimso Indian defense?

4. A jackknife and a good set of teeth are required for this youthful competition.

5. If you heard "his heels" or "his knobs," what game would you be playing?

6. Can you define the means of winning at jackstraws?

7. In this Japanese game, two players place counters on a multi-squared board. Five in a row wins. What is the game?

8. When you hit one end of a tapered piece of wood, send it upward, and hit it again for distance, what are you playing?

9. To our ancestors, flapdragon (or snapdragon) surely wasn't a flower. Do you know what it was?

10. For this Chinese game, you can use cards or beans and guess, or you can get rid of all you have to win.

GAMES III

answers

1. Clue.

2. King of diamonds.

3. In a chess match.

4. Mumblety-peg is the game. A jackknife is tossed from several positions and has to land upright with the blade stuck in the ground. In some versions, the loser has to pull a peg from the ground with his teeth.

5. The card game cribbage. In this competition, pegs are placed on a board to keep score. Heels and knobs are phrases associated with scoring procedures.

6. A pile of straws or wood strips is made. To succeed, players try to remove single pieces without moving the others. In a given time period, the player with the most pieces removed wins.

7. Gobang (Japanese: *goban*, chessboard).

8. Tip cat.

9. Before TV and radio, our ancestors challenged themselves to snatch raisins and/or other sweets from serving bowls filled with flaming brandy. The ol' "dragon" singed some chins. But the ol' brandy was a soothing balm.

10. Fan-tan (Chinese: *fan*, number of times + *t'an*, apportion). It is a gambling game in which players wager on the number of beans remaining in a pile that has been counted off in fours. It is also a card game with players discarding cards in proper sequence. the winner is the one who gets rid of his hand first.

GEMSTONES

Symbols of marriage or objects of greed, gemstones sparkle like the stars and countless sunpoints on the ocean tides. Will your score glisten, be considered precious, or be a real jewel in this quiz?

1. What anniversary is represented by the ruby?
2. What color is amber?
3. How many milligrams are there in a carat?
4. Besides carat weight, what are the other three C's of gems?
5. Which is the most dense of all gems?
6. What are American, twentieth century, and briolette?
7. Can you name the two stones that are forms of corundum and that vary only in color? What are these colors?
8. How does the Mohs scale relate to gems and minerals?
9. What mine was "Diamond" Jim Brady's source of wealth?
10. From what stone was the world's largest diamond, the Star of Africa, cut?

GEMSTONES

answers

1. The fortieth.

2. Yellow.

3. There are 200 milligrams.

4. Color, cut, and clarity.

5. The tinstone. It is also called cassiterite or native tin dioxide.

6. Types of gem cuts.

7. Rubies (red) and sapphires (deep blue).

8. Named after German mineralogist Friedrich Mohs, it is a scale indicating relative hardness, arranged in ten ascending degrees.

9. No mine was his source. Jim Brady gained his wealth by working for and with the massive development of railroads in the United States in the 1800s. He used diamonds as favors, gifts, and even tips, which established his nickname.

10. The Cullinan stone, which was discovered at the Premier Mine 2 in 1905 near Pretoria, South Africa.

GEOGRAPHY (U.S.)

Geography is one school subject that can be very fascinating if taught by a good teacher. If you had a poor instructor, take heart. The following are meant to rekindle your curiosity.

1. It is rightfully called the Green Mountain State.

2. This waterway was the eastern starting point for the Erie Canal.

3. Which is the only one of the Great Lakes that is completely within U.S. boundaries?

4. There are 46 boiling springs in this national park. What is the park and what state is it in? *Clue:* The park isn't Yellowstone.

5. Can you name the three main U.S. Virgin Islands? What is their capital?

6. What are the unique geographic features of Point Barrow in Alaska and Etta in the Aleutian Islands?

7. Which of Niagara's Falls is higher? And while we're there, from where does the Niagara River flow?

8. What site with a "western" name is the easternmost point in the United States?

9. Denver is known as the Mile High City, but it is not the highest city in the United States. What city is?

10. Where in the country is the John Muir Trail?

GEOGRAPHY (U.S.)

answers

1. Vermont.

2. The Hudson River.

3. Lake Michigan.

4. Hot Springs National Park in Akansas.

5. St. Croix, St. Thomas, and St. John. Their capital is Charlotte Amalie.

6. They are our northernmost and westernmost cities.

7. The American Falls is 167 feet high. The Canadian, or Horseshoe Falls, is 158 feet high. The Niagara river flows from Lake Erie into Lake Ontario.

8. The West Quoddy Head lighthouse on a peninsula of Quoddy Head State Park in Maine.

9. Leadville, Colorado, is America's highest incorporated city at two miles above sea level.

10. It is a beautiful nature trail that follows a route from Mt. Whitney to the Yosemite Valley in California.

GEOGRAPHY (WORLD)

From Kalamazoo to Katmandu, the world is filled with countless curiosities. So get your baggage checked and your tickets ready. Here we go!

1. Tweeds, twills, and tartans can be found in this Gaelic-speaking country.
2. Located on the prime meridian, this English city is the key point for the world's timekeepers.
3. What stretches through seven nations and is nicknamed Boat of Snow?
4. Known as the Land of the Rattlesnake, this nation has most of this reptile's recognized species.
5. Is Bali Ha'i (from the musical *South Pacific*) an actual island located in that region?
6. World War I troops sang that it was a "long way to Tipperary." Where is it?
7. Which volcanic peak in the Andes is South America's highest mountain?
8. Smaller than Washington, D.C., this nation is found between Austria and Switzerland. Name it and its capital.
9. Speaking of small and proud countries, which nation-state can be found in the Pyrenees Mountains on the French and Spanish border? Identify its capital also.
10. Do you remember the phrase Kalamazoo to Timbuktu? Kalamazoo is in Michigan. Was Timbuktu just a rhyme word?

GEOGRAPHY (WORLD)

answers

1. Scotland.

2. Greenwich, a borough of London. Its location at 0° longitude makes its location the basis for setting mean solar time.

3. The Himalayas.

4. Mexico.

5. Yes. It is the real island of Mooréa. It can be found northwest of the tropical paradise Tahiti.

6. Ireland. It is a town in a county of the same name in the south-central province of Munster.

7. Aconcagua. Located in Western Argentina, it rises to a height of 23,080 feet.

8. Liechtenstein. Vaduz is its capital and its area is 65 square miles.

9. Andorra. Andorra is also its capital city and its area is 191 square miles.

10. On the contrary, it's a real city in Mali, a country in western Africa. Its capital is Bamako and its area is 464,873 square miles.

GLITTERS (ALL THAT DOES)

From secret jewel caches to tales of buried treasure, here are additional facts about humankind's quest for all that glitters and some items that—well, see for yourself.

1. Can you name the object of medieval alchemists' obsessive desires and why it was sought?

2. Why has such a simple mineral like iron pyrite made fools out of so many people?

3. What revered President's wife contributed portions of her silver service for the first U.S. coins?

4. Alchemists' efforts are often mocked as ridiculous. However, they did discover three powerful acids in their misguided quest. Can you name them?

5. Why are cultured pearls not as "refined" as their name might indicate?

6. Who or what was the Welcome Stranger and why was this stranger so welcome indeed?

7. Though James Marshall found California gold near John Sutter's mill, it was a U.S. President who actually caused the 1849–1850 gold rush by announcing the find. Who was he?

8. Nicknamed the Watermelon, this stone has a green "skin" and is usually red inside.

9. Why would finding a modern-day philosopher's stone be a potential economic failure?

10. How did an emerald ring make a "derelict" of a British naval commander in 1707?

GLITTERS (ALL THAT DOES)

answers

1. The philosopher's stone. Alchemists believed it could help them change lead into gold.

2. It is iron sulfide, a lustrous yellowish metal. Though it serves as a source of sulfur, it is better known as fool's gold.

3. Martha Washington made this contribution.

4. Sulfuric, nitric, and hydrochloric.

5. This type of pearl is produced by placing a precut bead into the pearl-bearing mollusks. Such beads must be labeled as cultured before they're sold.

6. Found near Ballarat, Australia, in 1869, it was the largest gold nugget ever discovered and weighed almost 200 pounds.

7. President James K. Polk literally "poked into" the prospecting business when he announced the find in December of 1948 (half a year later).

8. The tourmaline. It is one of a group of complex silicates used as gems or in optical instruments.

9. Turning lead into gold today might very well swamp the market and thus make gold much less precious.

10. Admiral Cloudesley Shovel was fleet commander when his ship wrecked on the Scilly Island shoals in 1707. As he struggled ashore, he was murdered by a woman for his emerald ring. She justified her crime according to coast area beliefs that a washed-up body was a derelict with no legal rights. This excuse did not satisfy the hangman.

GRAB BAG

From garage sales to community bazaars, you can find a grab bag of items and surprises. Here are some facts that defy categorization, and sometimes logic too.

1. This word can mean a printer's apprentice or a fierce animal in Tasmania.

2. This word defines a type of macaroni or a pipe joint.

3. Can you name the substance that serves as a base for paint, is called wool wax, and comes from sheep's wool?

4. When a woman is knighted, what is she called?

5. What is the more common name for rhinoplastic surgery?

6. Why was Hobson's Choice really not a choice at all?

7. This famous historic site was once named the Flavian Amphitheater.

8. It means "sea foam" in German and is a popular pipemaking material.

9. To which fairy tale did the Folkething belong?

10. Speaking of such tales, how were they related to the popular antiquities of earlier centuries?

GRAB BAG

answers

1. Devil.

2. Elbow.

3. Lanolin.

4. Dame (Latin: *domina*, lady).

5. A nose job.

6. Thomas Hobson, a stable owner in Cambridge, England, rented horses in a rigid order according to their proximity to his front door. Thus, he created a "take it or leave it" decision for any renter and no real choice at all.

7. The Roman Colosseum.

8. Meerschaum.

9. To none of them. The Folkething is the Unicameral Legislature of Denmark.

10. Popular antiquities was the name for folklore *before* 1846. Folklore was suggested by William Thoms, a collector of such tales. The term fairy tale, however, existed as early as 1750 in the works of Horace Walpole, an English writer.

HALLS OF ACADEME

Enter the ivy-covered portals and walk carefully down these revered corridors. Whisper your answers, since you may be disturbing a budding Einstein.

1. Can you name the oldest university in the United States?

2. Who was the founder of Tuskegee Institute?

3. What was the predominant color of America's one-room schoolhouses, and why was that so?

4. Where was the site of the original Academe?

5. How did the "town and gown" battle of 1354 rock the walls of Oxford?

6. Which university stretches across four time zones?

7. Who taught and who received instruction in the "college of one"?

8. How does a Japanese student "volunteer" for medical school?

9. What was Ellen Swallow Richards's unique contribution to educational history?

10. What is the curriculum in the "School of the Ten Bells"?

HALLS OF ACADEME

answers

1. Harvard. It was founded at Cambridge, Massachusetts, in 1636.

2. Booker T. Washington founded it in 1881.

3. Red. This was the least costly color available since large quantities of the pigment could be made inexpensively.

4. In a grove near ancient Athens where Plato taught.

5. This tragic campus riot originated in a tavern quarrel. The violence lasted for three days in the Oxford area and resulted in several fatalities.

6. The University of Alaska. It encompasses four time zones—from a college in Kitchikan near British Columbia to a learning center on Adak in the Aleutians.

7. In her book *Beloved Infidel,* Sheilah Graham was the "pupil" of F. Scott Fitzgerald.

8. A Japanese student may have to provide as much as $100,000 in "voluntary gifts" to faculty members even to have an application considered. Such gift exchanges have become customary over the centuries in many aspects of Japanese life.

9. In 1873 she received a BS from MIT and thus became the first American woman to graduate from a scientific school.

10. This is an infamous "underground school" for pickpockets. A "graduate" must pick all ten pockets of a mannequin without ringing the bells that have been sewn into each pocket.

H-E-E-ERE'S MERV GRIFFIN

Merv Griffin is one of the top-level television communications and entertainment personalities. Yet as prominent as he is, how much can you say that you know about him? Let's take a closer look at his varied and interesting background.

1. Who was his most popular co-host?

2. Can you name Merv's long-time musical conductor?

3. What was Merv's profession in his early twenties?

4. What do *Word for Word*, *Jeopardy!*, and *Wheel of Fortune* have in common with Merv?

5. What game show did Merv once host in the early 1960s?

6. During which year did Merv first guest-host a major TV show, and which one was it?

7. Which 1968 street scene program was one of his most-watched broadcasts?

8. We're quite familiar with Merv's theme shows. Identify one of his earliest and most clever themes. *Clue*: More stars than usual shone that night.

9. What "bunch" gave Merv and the Freddy Martin Orchestra a 1950 Hit Parade multimillion seller?

10. Name the station (and the location) where Merv's professional radio career began in 1944.

H-E-E-ERE'S MERV GRIFFIN

answers

1. Arthur Treacher. He began his career as A. T. Veary in British films. He joined Merv in the mid-1960s and had a successful TV career to add to his previous credits.

2. He is the talented musician Mort Lindsey.

3. He sang with the Freddy Martin Orchestra.

4. All are TV quiz programs produced by Merv Griffin Productions.

5. He was the host of *Play Your Hunch*.

6. In 1962 he was the guest host for Jack Paar on *The Tonight Show.* His success that night was a great advancement in his career.

7. It was his program televised from Harlem. In that troubled summer, the show proved a bold and eventually very meaningful broadcast.

8. It was a gala salute to the stars of the silent screen era, with several of that period's luminaries in attendance.

9. It was the best-selling tune "I've Got a Lovely Bunch of Coconuts."

10. The station was KFRC in San Francisco.

H-E-E-ERE'S MERV GRIFFIN (ENCORE)

Yes, Merv Griffin has had many performance successes. Here are more encore entries from his varied career.

1. Who rightfully could claim to be Griffin's most loyal fan—based on sheer attendance records alone?

2. What now-famous movie star gives credit for his rapid career boost to humorous interviews with Merv? *Clue:* He played a television detective in the 1960s.

3. Which form of entertainment marketing, often associated with reruns, enabled *The Merv Griffin Show* to return to TV with all new programming in the mid-1960s?

4. In a famous meeting among Griffin, Clint Eastwood, and the Maharishi Mahesh Yogi, what surprise did Eastwood present to the Maharishi?

5. What do *Finian's Rainbow, The Moon Is Blue,* and *Come Blow Your Horn* have in common?

6. What "pointed" phrase did Arthur Treacher often use in his introductions?

7. Griffin had a role that once put him close to beastly murders, and in a recent release he was a comedic villain. Name both films.

8. Can you name the 1963 anagram game show that put a new word in Griffin's credits?

9. Which cowboy star of the 1920s and 1930s accidentally treated Griffin's TV set like a Western barroom and reset the scenery?

10. What dual significance did Studio 6B at NBC in New York have for Merv in April of 1962.

H-E-E-ERE'S MERV GRIFFIN (ENCORE)

answers

1. The one and only Mrs. Miller.

2. Burt Reynolds is the star. His visits enabled him to display a sense of comedy that surprised critics and audiences alike. Soon his career skyrocketed.

3. Syndication is the marketing form. In 1964 Griffin and Westinghouse Broadcasting made a successful deal that enabled new programming to be placed in time spots that most appealed to stations and their viewers in different regions.

4. Eastwood presented him with a red rose, since he admires the Maharishi and transcendental meditation.

5. They are plays in which the versatile Griffin performed at various stages of his career.

6. Treacher's introduction was frequently stated, "Look sharp now . . . and here is the dear fellow himself, M-e-r-v-y-n-!"

7. The beastly murders occurred in *Phantom of the Rue Morgue.* Recently Griffin delighted movie audiences as the sinister "elevator murderer" in *The Man with Two Brains.*

8. It was *Word for Word* and he became its producer.

9. Ken Maynard was the man. At the age of seventy, he chose to leave the stage for a break and in doing so separated a set that several stagehands had put together.

10. At Studio 6B, Merv taped his game show *Play Your Hunch* in the morning. In the evening, he was *The Tonight Show*'s guest host in the same studio.

HOAXES (SWINDLES AND PRACTICAL JOKES)

It seems that the gullible and the foolhardy have always been with us. though some of the following events and/or discoveries seem to be sure shams, don't remove your thinking cap until you're certain about the answer.

1. Which circus impresario was considered a "master trickster" by some?

2. How does the Latin phrase *cavoat emptor* relate to all potential ripoffs?

3. Unearthed in 1869 in New York State, this discovery has been called everything from the Great Onondaga to a petrified Phoenician idol. How is this twelve-foot figure better known today?

4. Can you explain how a dirty-digited toad ruined a man who once was called the "modern Darwin"?

5. He was known as "The Great Imposter" for assuming roles in several professions. A 1961 movie was based on his life.

6. There actually is a word, roorback, in standard dictionaries. Can you define it and explain how it damaged a presidential candidate?

7. How was the man known as the "Twentieth Century Vermeer" forced to admit one kind of crime in order to avoid a far harsher punishment?

8. What was the "turnip patch" Venus that shocked the art world in 1938?

9. How did the prankster Thomas Hook win a bet by making an unknown London street famous in one day in 1810?

10. In the 1870s, how did a double-named English Lord fleece some of America's biggest tycoons and nearly steal a railroad by using stolen diamonds?

HOAXES (SWINDLES AND PRACTICAL JOKES)

answers

1. Phineas Taylor Barnum.
2. *Caveat emptor* in Latin means "let the buyer beware."
3. It is known as the Cardiff Giant. Found in Cardiff, New York, some believed it was the remains of an Onondaga Indian prophet. A Yale paleontologist exposed it as a statue of gypsum. A tobacconist, George Hull, set up the scheme to make money and to hoodwink an evangelist with whom he had argued.
4. Viennese scientist Dr. Paul Kammerer claimed to have shown evidence of acquired characteristics in midwife toads. But the special egg-carrying trait of the male frogs was exposed as a fraud. The frogs' blackened thumb pads were found to have been injected with India ink and Kammerer lost his "Darwin" title.
5. He was Fred Demara, who impersonated business and professional people.
6. The word derived from a fictitious book, *Roorback's Tour Through the Western and Southern States in 1836*. A news article written by enemies of James K. Polk quoted from the book and claimed that "Mr. Roorback" had seen "43 slaves" branded with Polk's initials. Fortunately, Polk overcame this libel and won.
7. He was Hans van Meegeren. He was an art forger but had avoided arrest until being charged with the very serious crime of Nazi collaboration. He confessed to forgery to receive the lesser punishment.
8. A 1938 statue of Venus, minus its legs, nose, and an arm, was found in a French turnip patch and declared an art treasure. Then Italian Francesco Cremonse stepped forward with not only the missing parts but also the model, a nightclub singer.
9. He won a bet by making ordinary Berners Street the talk of London. On various pretexts, he managed to get several important officials, professional people, etc., to come to an unknowing woman's house. His friends aided by causing a traffic jam. The famous folks were seen and the uproar created a sensation.
10. He was Lord Gordon-Gordon. With money from an Edinburgh diamond theft, he secured credits, expense vouchers, and Erie Railroad stock. He bought, sold, and bought again until Jay Gould exposed him. Gordon fled into Canada and committed suicide in a Toronto cottage.

HOAXES (SWINDLES AND PRACTICAL JOKES) II

The foolhardy and gullible are still with us. Thus, the list of scams and schemes continues.

1. Which New York structure is often referred to when describing unsound deals and/or unwary buyers?

2. What famous 1938 radio report of an invasion could be called the hoax that panicked America?

3. Among his many curious presentations, P. T. Barnum once had an Egress. Can you describe this creature? *Clue:* There is a bird called an Egret which is a type of heron.

4. Forty-three years after the Great Onondaga was found, another strange, manlike being's remains were discovered in 1912 in England. For 41 more years, scientists were puzzled by it. Can you name this famous find?

5. What well-known but still successful swindle involves a prisoner, the post office, and a secret treasure?

6. How did the "Mulligan Letters" muddle the Presidential nomination of Republican James G. Blaine in 1876?

7. In 1835, what in the Universe happened when a newspaper, the New York *Sun*, and a possible precursor of Batman were linked in a "full Moon" story?

8. How did a vice suppressor, whispering children, and an anonymous tip enable a less than immodest painting to become a sensation?

9. What "Moral of the Whole" in the New York *Herald* caused a near panic in 1874?

10. Which "history" about a common bathroom fixture has become the most widespread "fact" of all?

HOAXES (SWINDLES AND PRACTICAL JOKES) II

answers

1. It is the Brooklyn Bridge.
2. It was *The War of the Worlds* radio adaptation of the famous novel. Many who listened to Orson Welles's team thought that Martians had invaded.
3. There is a heron called an egret. However, an egress is an exit. P.T. put up a sign reading, "This way to the egress." Many folks expected to find much more.
4. The Piltdown Man fooled many "experts." Englishman Charles Dawson, seeking antiquarian fame, created this "find" from a human skull and an orangutan's jaw. 1953 chemical tests lifted the veil of the fraud.
5. It is the "Mexican prisoner game." In it and similar versions, an "unjustly" imprisoned person in a foreign country sends a letter seeking help. This captive supposedly has a fortune being held in the U.S. To release the treasure and the prisoner, the person receiving the letter must send money to the address of one of the captive's friends (who is aiding his or her release).
6. The letters supposedly proved that Mr. Blaine had been helping certain railroads in exchange for bribes. Though they were false, they helped spoil his nomination bid.
7. The *Sun*'s "full Moon" hoax was concocted by young news reporter Richard Locke. He wrote about an Englishman who had seen batlike Moonmen with a new telescope. The sensational article accomplished its goal of increasing circulation (for a time).
8. Press agent Harry Reichenbach made a scandal and a real success of *September Morn.* He paid some children to whisper and giggle at the painting in a store's window. A tip to vice rules enforcer Anthony Comstock led to an investigation, an art dealer's trial, and history.
9. The *Herald* carried a shocking article about wild animals escaping from the Central Park Zoo. However, it ended with a disclaimer saying the report was a fictitious way of exposing the zoo's problems. One had to read the full or *whole* report to understand its meaning.
10. H. L. Mencken created the bathtub's history by placing its first use at an 1842 Cincinnati, Ohio, stag party. Though this was a practical joke in the 1917 New York *Evening Mail*, Mencken's "facts" began to appear in a number of scholarly articles, speeches, and books.

HODGE-A-PODGE

A hodgepodge is defined as (a) a thick stew of various meats and vegetables and (b) a jumbled mixture. This hodge-a-podge is an even thicker mix. So, trivia tasters, grab your forks and enjoy the feast!

1. If a CB fan has "bubble trouble," what is the problem?
2. This life preserver, worn by aviators downed at sea, was named after a shapely actress who wanted men to come up to see her.
3. You know that snake eyes are double aces thrown in dice. But can you define an ambsace?
4. COLA in a contract means something far different from a soft drink to an employee. What is it?
5. Can you name the first man-made object to break the sound barrier?
6. When a man in Scotland puts one foot on the dinner table, is he ordering dessert, relaxing, or making a taunting challenge, or doing something else altogether?
7. What is a Gentoo to a Moslem in India?
8. If your diamond ring lacked bezels, would it really be lacking anything?
9. In the 1930s if you didn't know the local speakeasy required a shibboleth, what could you have done?
10. If you know what a shibboleth is, do you have any idea where it originated?

HODGE-A-PODGE

answers

1. Tire problems.

2. Mae West.

3. It is another name for the lowest number thrown.

4. It is an acronym for the cost of living allowance, a very important matter to any working person.

5. A whip. The cracking sound is actually the breaking of the sound barrier with the whip's snapping speed.

6. Doing something else. He is proposing a toast.

7. A Hindu. Hindus are Gentiles to the Moslems.

8. It certainly would. Bezels are the slanting surfaces of a cut jewel, especially the upper half.

9. You could have taken a tug on your hip flask if you had one. Without the shibboleth, or password, your entry was denied in many "whoopie parlors."

10. It was a "pass the test" word used in the Bible (Judges 12:6). The Gileadites used it to trap the escaping Ephraimites, who could not pronounce the *sh*.

HORSE SMARTS

Surely you've heard of horse sense. Well, horse smarts is a variation of this. Grab the reins and test your brains with these.

1. Can you name the talking horse of 1960s television?
2. Can you name both the Lone Ranger's and Tonto's proud steeds?
3. Describe a yearling as it applies to racing.
4. Can you describe a hippocampus and explain what it is doing in this category?
5. Can you define a furlong and describe the origin of its meaning?
6. What was Eohippus?
7. Whose horse was Widowmaker and what great feat made both mount and rider legendary?
8. Define the terms "gee" and "haw" and describe when they are meant to be used.
9. Which was the first steed to win the Triple Crown?
10. Why weren't horses used for heavy farm work before the twelfth century?

HORSE SMARTS

answers

1. Mr. Ed.

2. Silver and Scout respectively.

3. It is a thoroughbred racehorse that is one year old or that has not completed its second year.

4. The hippocampus is a semitropical fish with foreparts and a head somewhat similar to a horse. After all—this section is for smart horses, isn't it?

5. It is an eighth of a mile, or 220 yards. (Anglo-Saxon: *fur*, a furrow + *lang*, long). Thus a furlong originally meant the length of a furrow.

6. Eohippus was the ancestor of today's horse. It was approximately the size of a fox and had toes instead of hoofs.

7. Pecos Bill was his master. Widowmaker promptly sent any unwanted riders for a fatal tumble, thus earning his name. Pecos Bill and his steed were the legendary creators of the Rio Grande and other Western wonders.

8. They are commands to horses or oxen being driven without reins. Gee means "turn right." Haw means "turn left."

9. Sir Barton in 1919.

10. The chest harness, which had been used since Roman times, was inefficient. The invention of the horse collar (or shoulder harness) made pulling farm implements practical.

HOW 'BOUT THAT!

Pshaw, doggone, and fiddlesticks! Here's more of them thar consarned, galldanged brain benders to muddle the minds of even a cracker-barrel sage!

1. Founded in 1867, this farmers' organization was also known as the Patrons of Husbandry.
2. What is the name for a young cow that has never borne a calf?
3. This means of illumination Is also a method of embroidering muslin. What is the common factor in both?
4. When folks sweat out a fire-and-brimstone homily, what more common term have they been hearing?
5. What do strap, T, and spring have in common?
6. The 4-H Clubs have many creative, farsighted members. Can you identify the H's?
7. What did a person possess if he had a large supply of Attic salt?
8. This agrarian-backed political party advocated free coinage, publicly owned utilities, and an income tax.
9. What is the name for the tobacco that remains in a pipe's bowl after smoking?
10. Is it colder in the country than it is in the winter?

HOW 'BOUT THAT!

answers

1. The Grange. It was organized by farmers for mutual advancement and protection.

2. A heifer.

3. It is a candle's wick or the method of candlewick.

4. A sermon. Homiletics is the art of writing and preaching sermons.

5. They are all types of hinges.

6. Head, heart, hands, and health.

7. He certainly did not have an upper room full of sodium chloride. Rather, he was quite witty. Attic in this case is derived from Attica, a region of ancient Greece. Many people of that nation were noted for their grace, appreciation of the arts, and cultured lives. Thus a person having Attic salt was considered witty and wise.

8. It was the People's party (1891–1904). Its members were called Populists.

9. Dottle, or dottel. (Do tell!)

10. Of course, not necessarily, or at all. If you missed this one, don't worry. Just keep studying and someday you'll have the number one chair between the potbellied stove and the cracker barrel!

IN OUR CUPS

Whether it was the nectar of the gods or the W.C. Fields's type of movie tippling, people have always had a thirst for finding and sampling all kinds of brew. However, there is a darker side to beverage indulgence. In all fairness to nonimbibers, we offer the following choices.

1. Upon which vehicle do reforming victims of "demon rum" often have to ride?
2. When someone goes out to paint the town, what is another name for the "curving" way he goes?
3. What word often used for nondrinkers mistakenly suggests that tea is the main selection of the abstainers?
4. Which Carrie carried a hatchet in her temperance quest?
5. In a starkly realistic 1945 movie, what period of time did the dipsomaniac misplace?
6. We know that Prohibition (1920–1933) forbade the manufacture, transport, and sale of alcohol. However, what key factor did it not prohibit? Also, what was the official name for the law that was used in the attempt to enforce Prohibition?
7. Was the first abstinence organization the Anti-Saloon League, the American Society for the Promotion of Temperance, or the Woman's Christian Temperance Union?
8. In the classic 1870s barroom story, how many nights were involved in the tragic tale?
9. In the perception of artist William Hogarth, why wasn't the *Rake's Progress* an advance after all?
10. How did Rutherford B. Hayes's wife acquire the nickname Lemonade Lucy?

IN OUR CUPS

answers

1. It is the wagon. (Many have fallen off this vehicle and have found themselves in the "paddy wagon.")

2. The "curve" is also known as a bender. (This direction is often taken in the questionable company of that perpetual rounder John Barleycorn.)

3. The word is teetotaler. Actually, this word was derived from teetotal, a colloquialism that meant entire or complete. Thus a complete abstainer was a teetotaler.

4. The lady was Carrie Nation, born Carrie Amelia Moore. Her family's bouts with whisky problems led her to some excesses in swinging her hatchet.

5. *The Lost Weekend.* Ray Milland received an Oscar for his performance in this film version of Charles Jackson's book.

6. It did not prohibit the drinking of liquor. The law was the Volstead Act, named after Representative Andrew J. Volstead. He was a Republican from Minnesota who served in Congress from 1903 to 1923.

7. It was the American Society for the Promotion of Temperance founded in 1826. The Woman's Christian Temperance Union originated in 1874 and the Anti-Saloon League began in 1895.

8. There were ten nights. Timothy Shay Arthur's popular *Ten Nights in a Barroom* was "must" reading for the temperance movement. A tragic account of a once-prosperous man's demise, the book was dramatized as a play.

9. In Hogarth's painted version, the Rake "progressed" along Gin Lane to temptations and eventual ruin.

10. After President Hayes forbade alcoholic beverages in the White House in 1877, his wife, Lucy, frequently served Roman punch. It consisted of lemon juice, sugar, and egg whites.

INDIANS

Often misinterpreted and misrepresented, the Indian people have a truly proud history. The following facts are but a sample of their glorious traditions.

1. She saved Captain John Smith. However, it was as another man's wife that she became the rage of old London town.

2. This Sioux chief did far more than win a battle in 1876 against the reckless "Golden Hair."

3. In *The Song of Hiawatha* by Longfellow, who was the Daughter of the Moon named Nokomis?

4. She was the mother of a famous British statesman and was one-eighth Iroquois. She attributed her abundant energy to this ancestry.

5. Of which people was Atahualpa a ruler?

6. How do Indians use a calumet?

7. What are the three most populous U.S. Indian tribes?

8. The Hopi settlement of Old Oraibi in Arizona is considered by many to be the oldest occupied settlement in the United States, dating from A.D. 1100. Besides its age, what is unique about Old Oraibi?

9. Who played the role of Pahookatawah, friend of Yancy Derringer, in the television series?

10. Which son of a full-blooded Kaw Indian served as U.S. Vice President from 1929 to 1932?

INDIANS

answers

1. She was Pocahontas, an Algonquian Indian princess. As Mrs. John Rolphe, she was a sensation in London and charmed everyone at court.

2. He was Sitting Bull. As chief of the Sioux, he capably led his people for many years through everything from blizzards to famine.

3. She was Hiawatha's grandmother.

4. She was Winston Churchill's mother, Jennie Jerome of New York, who married Randolph Churchill.

5. Atahualpa was the last Inca king in Peru.

6. They smoke it. A calumet is a peace pipe.

7. They are the Navaho, Cherokee, and Sioux respectively.

8. The Hopi tribe doesn't permit visitors to the settlement.

9. He was an Indian actor named X. Brands.

10. He was Charles Curtis, who served with Herbert Hoover. Before 1929, he had been a senator and congressman from Kansas.

IS THAT SO?

Even the most dedicated scholars acquire a certain number of misconceptions among facts, factoids, and fancy. Here is a compilation that may surprise you and save you from a crushing cocktail party faux pas. These may be answered True or False.

1. King John sealed the Magna Carta in 1215.
2. St. Patrick was the first Irish saint to be born in his native Ireland.
3. Cape Agulhas, not the Cape of Good Hope, is actually the southernmost tip of Africa.
4. In the song "Home on the Range," the antelope is wrongly depicted as playing there.
5. The so-called sound you hear in a seashell is always anything but the sea.
6. Contrary to historical revisionists' research, the six-gun really did win the West.
7. Prince Henry the Navigator was not the seaman he was reputed to be.
8. Steam is not wet.
9. There are no phone books in Russia's phone booths.
10. In our universe, if an immovable object were struck by an irresistible force, a cataclysm similar to an atomic explosion would occur.

IS THAT SO?

answers

1. *True*. King John did not know how to write and made the document official with his seal.

2. *False*. Saint Patrick wasn't Irish. He was British and was the victim of Irish raiders who kidnapped him to the Emerald Isle.

3. *True*. Cape Agulhas is correct. It is some 35 miles farther south than the Cape of Good Hope.

4. *True*. There are no species of antelope roaming freely on North American ranges. The animal to which the song may have referred is the pronghorn. It combines some features of the deer, giraffe, goat, antelope, and sheep.

5. *False*. It could be the sea if you were near a shoreline. Actually, you could hear a number of nearby sounds, including the blood passing along the veins of your ear. The shell's shape permits noises to echo while the air in the shell vibrates.

6. *False*. The revisionists are right. The six-gun was only one factor in winning the West. Others incude better land management, the steel plow, dynamite, and barbed wire.

7. *True.* History has no record of Henry's voyages. He received his title for his direction of the explorer's institute at Sagres, Portugal.

8. *True*. Steam isn't wet. In fact, it can be seen as a mist only when it meets cooler air. Condensation causes it to change into water drops. Only then is it "wet."

9. *True*. After all, Russia isn't known as a "paper tiger" police state. When the state is all-watching, it is all-listening too.

10. *False.* It would be impossible. In our universe, according to all known principles of science, if one exists (force or object), the other cannot.

JAPAN (AN ORIENTATION)

This nation of many mysteries has come a long way since the days when the phrase "made in Japan" meant poor quality. Now the Japanese are world-ranked producers in a number of economic sectors. What do you know about one of America's chief competitors?

1. What was the name of Japan's ancient warrior-rulers?

2. What is Japan's best-known and most photographed peak?

3. Why is the Ginza district famous?

4. Which of Japan's islands is its largest?

5. Who in Japan might be called an "art person"?

6. In many war documentaries, Japanese soldiers are shown shouting, "Banzai!" Do you know what it means?

7. What Japanese attack on a Russian port presaged Pearl Harbor by 37 years?

8. Why are there no rooms with the number 9 in many Japanese hotels and hospitals?

9. A kimono is a garment. What is a kakemono?

10. What famous event occurred in March of 1853 at Shimoda, Japan, and how was the brother of an American hero involved?

JAPAN (AN ORIENTATION)

answers

1. Shoguns. They ruled as military governors of Japan and relegated many of the emperors to lesser positions.

2. Mt. Fujiyama, a volcanic peak near Tokyo.

3. It is a popular shopping and entertainment center.

4. Honshu, with an area of 91,278 square miles. Tokyo is located here.

5. A geisha (Japanese: *gei*, art + *sha*, person). Geishas are trained to entertain and converse with other people, mainly men.

6. It translates, "May you live ten thousand years!"

7. On February 6, 1904, at the outset of the Russo-Japanese War, Japanese destroyers surprised the Russian fleet at Port Arthur in northeastern China. Russian battleships were quickly sunk with torpedoes. Then, 37 years later, the Japanese used an aerial attack and torpedoes at Pearl Harbor. A tragic lesson of history had not been learned.

8. In Japan the word for *nine* sounds very much like the word for *suffering* and is thought inappropriate by many hotel and hospital administrators.

9. A kakemono is a hanging scroll of silk or paper with a picture or inscription and a roller at its base.

10. Commodore Matthew Calbraith Perry entered Shimoda and ceremoniously opened Japan to U.S. trade. He was the brother of naval hero Oliver Hazard Perry.

JAZZ (BLUES, RHYTHM, AND MORE)

Come on along to that special side-alley hideaway. You know the one. The smoke is thick and that saxophone is hot. So, friends, Americans, compatriots, lend me two ears!

1. This jazz great had her first hit record with "A Tisket a Tasket" in 1938.

2. Who was known as the Father of the Blues?

3. Who was known as the Empress of the Blues?

4. He was the King of Ragtime and also wrote an unusual opera. Can you name him and his opera?

5. Which group became noted for applying jazz to a concert format?

6. What kind of musician is prominently *featured* in the movies *Birth of the Blues*, *New Orleans*, and *Syncopation*?

7. Who was the legendary jazz cornetist and pianist whose greatest piano creation was "In a Mist"?

8. Can you locate and describe the importance of the jazz center called Storyville?

9. What made the jazz singer Lee Wiley unusual?

10. If you *split* a *gig* because the *bread* you got there didn't *cover the sting* for *grease*, what did you do?

JAZZ (BLUES, RHYTHM, AND MORE)

answers

1. Ella Fitzgerald.
2. W. C. Handy. He wrote such classics as "St. Louis Blues" and "Beale Street Blues."
3. Bessie Smith.
4. Scott Joplin. His opera was *Tremonisha*.
5. The Dave Brubeck Quartet.
6. A trumpet player.
7. Leon Bismark Beiderbecke (known as "Bix").
8. It was the well-known "red light" district of New Orleans in the early 1900s. Numerous jazz musicians played there. When the Navy ordered the area closed in 1917, many jazz greats moved to other cities and spread the popularity of jazz nationwide.
9. She was a blond American Indian singer and composer. Noted for a distinctive style, she was very popular in the 1940s.
10. You *left* a *job* because it didn't pay enough *money* for the *price* of *food.*

JAZZ JARGON

Jazz musicians have developed a style of language uniquely their own. Try your hand at "translating" these.

1. Bash
2. Gas
3. Fracture
4. Hacked
5. Hype
6. Woodshed
7. Dogtime
8. Snake
9. Fall by
10. Ax

JAZZ JARGON

answers

1. Party
2. Excite
3. Impress someone
4. Tired, exasperated
5. A kind of deception
6. Practice time (Yes, even jazz artists had to practice!)
7. A bad piece of music
8. Subway
9. Visit someone
10. Any work implement, such as a horn

JEOPARDIZE

Surely you remember *Jeopardy*, the long-running TV game show of the 1960s and 1980s in which contestants had to create questions from the answers given. Well, here is another version of that type of competition. Please read the answers, then carefully write your questions (1 to 10) on a piece of paper. Approximate variations will be acceptable.

1. They never copy each other's visages. They like to take pratfalls. A hobo named Willy represents them at their best.

2. They comprise some 16 percent of the toy market. Madame Alexander is one of their all-time favorites. A certain GI is another big seller.

3. This autumn holiday occurs during a month that is in the zodiac time of Sagittarius. Indians helped begin the tradition.

4. Immigrants in the early 1900s thought it was butter. It is part of a "Hoboken special."

5. European nations were beginning to interfere in Central and South America. The United States had to take a stand.

6. Potato starch, gum arabic, and penny black have affected their history.

7. It is a part of a large European nation. Important strategic events occurred here. Omaha, Juno, and Utah are associated with it.

8. It is 34 feet longer than the Eiffel Tower is high, has a Veranda Grill, and was retired in 1967.

9. He stood eighteen inches high but he often had an arm that was eight feet long.

10. Babylon's King Hammurabi decreed that all people should wear it. It can be natural or synthetic. It is tested at a workbench called an organ.

JEOPARDIZE

answers

1. Who are clowns?
2. What are dolls?
3. When is Thanksgiving?
4. What is ice cream?
5. Why was the Monroe Doctrine stated?
6. How did postage stamps develop?
7. Where is Normandy?
8. What was the *Queen Mary*?
9. Who was King Kong?
10. What is perfume?

KNICKKNACKS

Knickknacks are small, ornamental articles or contrivances, mere gimcracks or trinkets. Yet many folks have shelves filled with such items, which they treasure beyond measure. Consider the choices below and see where you would put them in your mind's cupboard.

1. If you were in the very populous country also known as Bhrat, where would you be?

2. These popular shoes in the late 1930s are also vehicles of portage on rivers.

3. When a mistigris is wild in the right card game, it can make you a quick winner. What is it?

4. They were a dynasty's guard dogs and they have oddly cute, wrinkled faces.

5. What role does Fannie Mae have in the U.S. government and why would anyone want to talk with her about loans?

6. Where would you find a sweet spot in sports?

7. How might a firefighter be turned out twice when an alarm goes in?

8. Do you really know the back of your hand that well? You do? Then what is its other name?

9. Who often wears a tallywhacker?

10. Where is the purlicle of the hand?

KNICKKNACKS

answers

1. In India.

2. Barges.

3. The good ol' joker.

4. The Shar-pei breed, which was developed originally during China's Han dynasty.

5. Fannie Mae is the FNMA, the Federal National Mortgage Association.

6. On a tennis racquet and a golf club. The sweet spot is the place to strike the ball for best results.

7. By being aroused, or "turned out," from slumber and by donning a working uniform known as a "turnout."

8. The opisthenar. When you know something as well as your opisthenar, you're in good shape.

9. A sailor. It is the flap of material across the back of the sailor's uniform.

10. It is the space between one's thumb and forefinger.

VISUAL QUIZ NUMBER THREE

L'EPÉE'S LANGUAGE

L'EPÉE'S LANGUAGE

Abbé de l'Epée, a French monk, is credited with devising a one-hand sign language for the deaf in 1775. The hand positions given herein are from his manual alphabet. Try them in this trivia quiz.

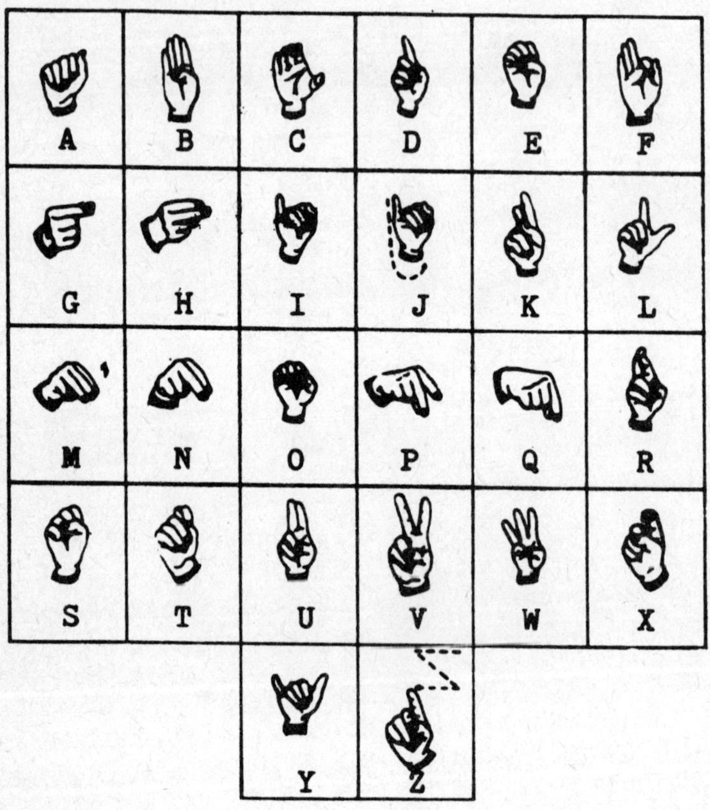

L'EPÉE'S LANGUAGE

Use your hands and thoughts to discern these signs. They stand for people who often use their hands—namely sports figures. Identify them and their best-known team. Jot down your answers for the code and the team "between the lines" and then turn the page to check them.

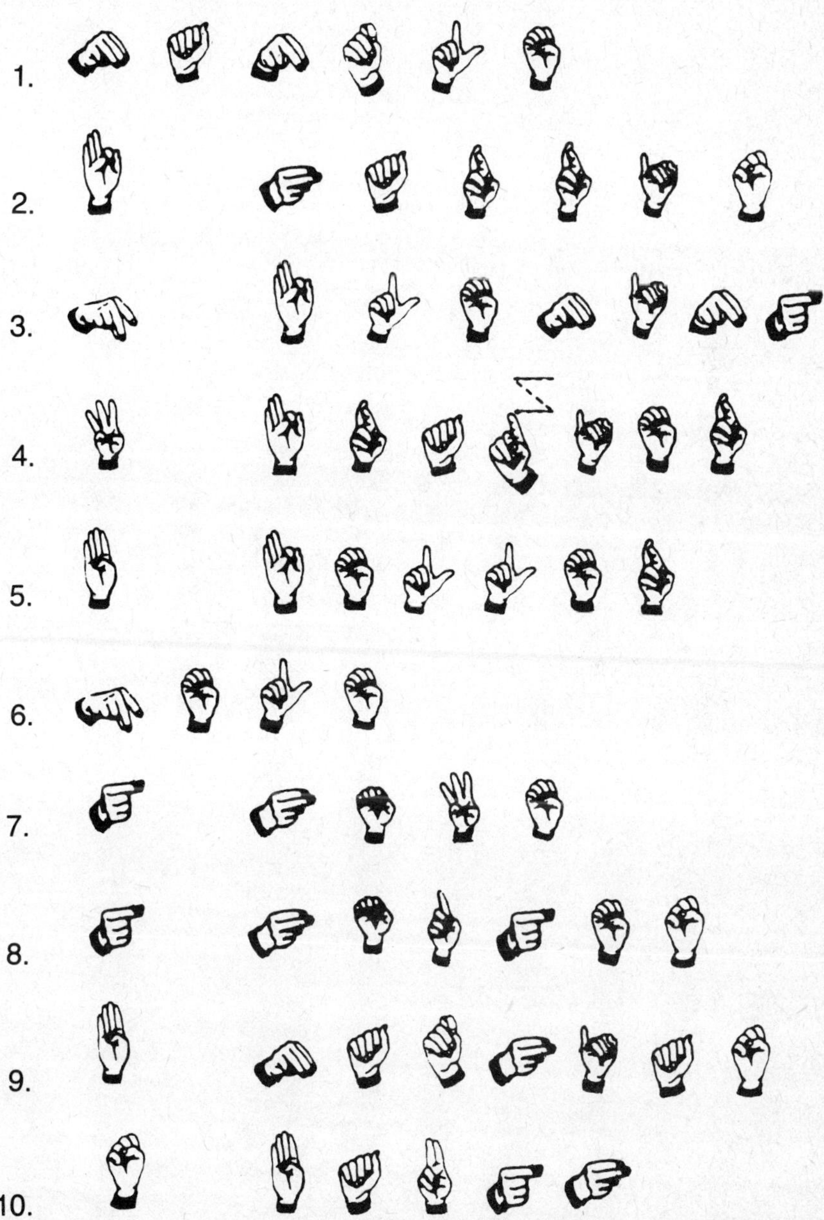

L'EPÉE'S LANGUAGE

answers

	CODE	TEAM
1.	Mantle (Mickey Mantle)	New York Yankees
2.	F. Harris (Franco Harris)	Pittsburgh Steelers
3.	P. Fleming (Peggy Fleming)	U.S. Olympic Team
4.	W. Frazier (Walt Frazier)	New York Knickerbockers
5.	B. Feller (Bob Feller)	Cleveland Indians
6.	Pele	New York Cosmos
7.	G. Howe (Gordie Howe)	Detroit Redwings
8.	G. Hodges (Gil Hodges)	Brooklyn Dodgers
9.	B. Mathias (Bob Mathias)	U.S. Olympic Team
10.	S. Baugh (Sammy Baugh)	Washington Redskins

LITERATURE

This segment includes facts from several types of literary works, including those from America, England, and other countries.

1. This famous Roman poet was the author of *The Aeneid*.

2. His pseudonym was O. Henry. What was his real name and for which writing style is he best remembered?

3. What was the "jungle" in Upton Sinclair's classic exposé novel *The Jungle*?

4. What puzzle is associated with the final novel of Charles Dickens?

5. Which American poetess became such a recluse that she spoke to her houseguests from another room?

6. What is the Edgar award and what master of a literary style is it named for?

7. In nineteenth-century Polynesia, who was known as Tusitala?

8. Which poem helped save a ship that had once defended America? Why was the ship in danger?

9. Which literary hero actually lived and was the first to propose space travel by rockets?

10. Who was the woman who wrote the oldest-known novel in the world—*The Tale of Genji*? Why was she not considered unique in her native land then?

LITERATURE

answers

1. Virgil.

2. He was William Sydney Porter. He is best remembered for short stories with surprise endings.

3. In particular, it was the Chicago stockyards circa 1906. In general, it was the horribly unclean condition of the U.S. food-processing industry. The novel caused a national outrage and led to constructive legislation.

4. His last novel was *The Mystery of Edwin Drood*. The puzzle concerns why the book was never finished. Some attempts have been made to complete it. However, even imitating Dickens is a monumental effort.

5. Emily Dickinson. Though she is highly regarded today, only seven of her poems were published in her lifetime.

6. The Edgar is given by the Mystery Writers of America for the year's best mystery. It is named for Edgar Allen Poe.

7. Tusitala is Polynesian for "teller of tales." It refers to Robert Louis Stevenson, who had a home there.

8. Oliver Wendell Holmes's *Old Ironsides.* The poem was about the U.S. frigate *Constitution*, which was about to be put on the scrap heap. The poem inspired a "penny drive" by millions of schoolchildren.

9. He was Cyrano de Bergerac, the true-life hero of an Edmond Rostand drama. A poet and adventurer, Cyrano studied the heavens as well.

10. She was Murasaki Shikibu. According to her diaries and other records, several women writers once existed in Japan. However, cultural and religious influences soon relegated women to subservient and less creative roles.

LITERATURE (ANOTHER CHAPTER)

Continue to turn, if you will, through this next collection of questions on thought-provoking pages, poets, and plays.

1. Set in Chicago, this Lorraine Hansberry play was a powerful depiction of the struggle for equality.

2. His stories were frequently set in Yoknapatawpha County and were as involved as the county name was to spell or pronounce.

3. *A Doll's House* is often described as an early "women's liberation" story. Do you know who wrote it?

4. Can you name the famous master work of adultery which, though "mild" today, caused near ruin for its author in France?

5. Who was Wilkie Collins and why were his novels considered of historic importance?

6. Can you name the central character in the classic novel *The Man Without a Country*?

7. When might the "divine prerogative" be applied in literature and who has the power to use it?

8. Who was America's first widely accepted novelist?

9. Which poet of ancient Crete not only fell asleep earlier than Rip Van Winkle but also outslept him?

10. Do tell—what is the *Book of Kells*?

LITERATURE (ANOTHER CHAPTER)

answers

1. It was *A Raisin in the Sun*.

2. He was William Faulkner.

3. It was written by Henrik Ibsen, a farsighted Norwegian dramatist and poet.

4. The book was *Madame Bovary*. In France in the 1850s, it was condemned as pornographic and led to much controversy. Its author was Gustave Flaubert.

5. William Wilkie Collins was an English novelist. His works *The Moonstone* and *The Woman in White* are accepted as the first full-length detective novels in the English language.

6. He was Philip Nolan. In the story by Edward Everett Hale, Nolan unwisely cursed the United States. He was condemned to a life at sea without news of America.

7. Authors use the "divine prerogative." Arthur Conan Doyle had Sherlock Holmes "killed" in a struggle with Professor Moriarty in the story "The Final Problem." Doyle had Sherlock Holmes "return" for the story "The Adventure of the Empty House." Thus writers use their prerogative or right to alter their characters and plots.

8. She was Susanna Rowson. Her book, *Charlotte Temple*, was published in 1791 and sold very well in every state.

9. His name was Epimenides. He lived in approximately 600 B.C. He told a tale of falling asleep for 57 years after hunting sheep. He outdozed ol' Rip by 37 years, give or take a few blinks.

10. It is a collection of Latin gospels. Dating from A.D. 700, it has classic Celtic artwork and is displayed at Dublin's Trinity College.

VISUAL QUIZ NUMBER FOUR

LUNAR
[MOON] TYPE

LUNAR (MOON) TYPE

The lunar type form was developed for people who become blind in adult life. It contains embossed or raised symbols that are similar to Roman capital letters. Though largely supplanted by Braille, it is a valued aid.

A	Λ
B	ɩ
C	C
D	Ɔ
E	Γ
F	ſ
G	ʔ
H	⊙
I	I
J	J
K	<
L	L
M	˥
N	N
O	O
P	ᓚ
Q	ᓗ
R	\
S	/
T	—
U	U
V	V
W	∩
X	>
Y	˩
Z	Z

LUNAR (MOON) TYPE

Now that you've seen the lunar style's chart, try linking these coded terms about the planets with the planets themselves. Jot down your answers for the code and the planet "between the lines" and then turn the page to check them.

1. O > ┘ ɿ ┌ N

2. \ I N ɿ /

3. C Λ N Λ L /

4. b ┌ Λ U – ┘

5. L Λ \ ɿ ┌ / –

6. / ┐ Λ L L ┌ / –

7. L Λ / –

8. / ┌ Λ   ɿ O Ɔ

9. / ┌ V ┌ N – ⊙

10. \ ┌ Ɔ   / ⊆ O –

LUNAR (MOON) TYPE

answers

	CODE	PLANET
1.	Oxygen	Earth
2.	Rings	Saturn
3.	Canals	Mars (once believed to have canals)
4.	Beauty	Venus (the Roman goddess reputedly was gorgeous)
5.	Largest	Jupiter
6.	Smallest	Mercury
7.	Last	Pluto
8.	Sea God	Neptune (named after the Roman sea god)
9.	Seventh	Uranus
10.	Red Spot	Jupiter

MATH MAZE

From 1 + 1 to the intricacies of Euclid, we've enjoyed numerical curiosities or suffered with seemingly insolvable muddles. Keep your gray-matter calculators or abacuses (abaci) handy as you enter this logarithmic labyrinth.

1. What number that meant so much to the original Colonies is also very prominent on the $1 bill?
2. What is absent from the Roman numeral system?
3. What single integer can be added to itself and can be multiplied with itself to get the same result? *Clue*: It isn't too difficult.
4. To whom should we give credit for the modern decimal system?
5. Simply, define a prime number.
6. To a mathematician, what does *i* mean?
7. Without being too loquaciously numerous, define the Fibonacci series.
8. Gosh, what's a googol?
9. Is there such a "what's it" as a perfect number?
10. Why does Pierre de Fermat's last theorem remain such a problem for mathematicians today?

MATH MAZE

answers

1. The number 13. Groups of 13s on the $1 bill include the pyramid's steps, the stars over the eagle's head, the stripes on the shield, the war arrows in the eagle's left talon, and the leaves on the olive branch in its right talon. There are 13 letters in each of the Latin phrases. Well, the printers certainly didn't seem superstitious!

2. The number 0. It comes from India by way of the Arabic system.

3. The number 2. For example: $2 + 2 = 4; 2 \times 2 = 4$.

4. The Hindus developed it around 800 B.C.. By this method, numerals with decimals indicated units, tens, hundreds, and so on—vast improvements over awkward Roman numerals.

5. Any number that can be divided by no other whole number than itself and 1.

6. It is the square root of -1. The concept is used in complex number theory in fields like electronics.

7. In this series, each number is equal to the sum of the preceding two. For example: $1 + 1 = 2; 1 + 2 = 3; 2 + 3 = 5$.

8. It is the number 1 followed by 100 zeroes. Or, it is the number 10 to the 100th power.

9. There certainly is. The Greeks determined 6 to be the first one. Such a number is the sum of its divisors (except itself). For example: $1 + 2 + 3 = 6$. Others include 78 and 8128.

10. Pierre de Fermat, a French mathematician, found that the equation $x^n + y^n = z^n$ did not have a solution in whole numbers except when $n = 2$. Therefore, $3^2 + 4^2 = 5^2$. Scholars have been trying in vain for centuries to find the proof.

MILITARY MATTERS

Whether in a mock survival game or on a checkerboard, many of us have imagined ourselves as strategists and leaders of great armies and armadas. Over the ages, such dreams of conquest have led to glorious victories or crushing defeats. Gather your mental forces now as we survey military secrets and surprises of the centuries.

1. She was the French peasant girl who stunned English generals with strategies from "afar."

2. Which emperor learned a terrible lesson that was ignored by a dictator 129 years later?

3. Who were the offspring of "Long Max" and "Big Bertha" and also unwanted guests in Paris in World War I?

4. We know about the Civil War clash between the *Monitor* and the *Merrimac*. However, do you know the *Merrimac*'s southern name?

5. What was the great misconception that was mounted at the time the Rough Riders fought in Cuba in 1898?

6. Which U.S. President has been the only one to pursue directly his position as commander-in-chief?

7. What single improvement of a riding implement enabled the T'ang dynasty's cavalry to extend its control from central China through much of Asia?

8. Regarding cavalry, how on earth did French soldiers on horseback capture a Dutch fleet in 1794?

9. What was the only force in the world to stop the Mongol army of Kublai Khan? How did the namesake of this power affect the U.S. military in World War II?

10. Besides Hannibal's exploits, can you name the only other famous "Battle of the Pachyderms"?

MILITARY MATTERS

answers

1. Jeanne d'Arc, Maid of Orleans. Better known as Joan of Arc, she led the French victory at Orleans, France. She believed that she was guided by visions and voices.

2. In 1812, Napoleon discovered too late the folly of invading Russia by land. By 1941, Adolph Hitler had failed to learn from this example and doomed his Nazi forces in World War II.

3. The "offspring" were shells fired at Paris by "Big Bertha" (a huge mortar) and "Long Max" (a long-barreled artillery piece). Obviously, the shells would never be "wanted."

4. The *Virginia*.

5. The Rough Riders weren't mounted when they fought to victory. Because of poor supply planning, their steeds arrived too late for the famous battle.

6. James Madison. In August of 1814, when British troops were attacking Washington, D.C., he took command of a gun battery at Bladensburg, Maryland. He continued his leadership until the situation became hopeless.

7. The invention of longer stirrups made for a steadier ride and greater maneuverability, both of which aided in warfare.

8. It wasn't on earth but, rather, on ice. The cavalry discovered a Dutch fleet icebound and surprised the crews on board by riding out to surround them.

9. The Mongols attacked Japan by sea but a hurricane wrecked their ships. The Japanese called the storm *kamikaze*, or "the divine wind." This same name was used for the Japanese suicide air force that attacked U.S. vessels in World War II.

10. In 217 B.C., during the Fourth Syrian War, the Syrian commander used Asian elephants to defeat the Egyptian army and its smaller North African elephants.

MILITARY MATTERS II

Here is another collection of military triumphs and debacles for all would-be field marshals and commodores to study.

1. How did both unrecognized radar "bleeps" and a telegram that arrived five hours late spell doom for an apparently safe fleet?

2. Which American hero who fled Great Britain after a fight later told the British that he had not yet begun to fight?

3. What war began after reconciliation had been sought and continued after a peace treaty was signed?

4. Which two nations signed the "Endless Peace Treaty" in A.D. 533 but found themselves fighting seven years later?

5. In 1905, what fleet sailed 18,000 miles for seven months only to be destroyed in a day?

6. How did fire and vinegar aid Hannibal's forces almost as much as his elephants did when he fought Rome?

7. The United States fought a war with Korea before the 1950s. Do you know the when and the why of it?

8. What do you know about the War of Jenkin's Ear?

9. How many troops were actually involved in the fourteenth-century Battle of the Thirty between England and France?

10. In the seventh and ninth centuries the Byzantine Empire used "Greek fire" to repel attacking Muslim invaders. What was Greek fire?

MILITARY MATTERS II

answers

1. On the morning of December 7, 1941, the Opana radar station on Hawaii's Kahuku Point picked up the "bleeps" of incoming planes 136 miles away. When the men on duty notified their superiors, the planes were mistaken as "friendly." Five hours after the Pearl Harbor disaster, a message from Washington sent by slower commercial telegram channels arrived to warn Hawaii's forces to be alert.
2. He was John Paul, who left England after being wrongly charged for killing a mutinous seaman. In the United States, he became John Paul Jones and a great hero.
3. The War of 1812 between Britain and America. The news of a withdrawal of troublesome British naval orders failed to arrive in the United States before war was declared. Similarly, reports of the peace treaty in 1815 were too late to stop the Battle of New Orleans.
4. The Roman Empire and Persia.
5. The sister fleet of the hapless Russian ships sunk at Port Arthur. This Russian Baltic fleet was annihilated in the Straits of Tsushima between Korea and Japan by the surprisingly strong Japanese.
6. Hannibal's military engineers heated immovable boulders with flaming logs. Then they poured vinegar on the rocks to split them into fragments for easier removal.
7. In 1871, Korea broke off trade with the United States. A month of warfare ended in a draw, though each side claimed victory. Eighty years later, U.S. and UN forces were again at war against the North Koreans, who had invaded South Korea.
8. Captain Robert Jenkins was the victim of a Spanish patrol in 1738 in the West Indies. He took his pickled, severed ear to Parliament and caused a furor. The British declared a war that later became named for the captain's ear.
9. Sixty men in all. In the fourteenth century, England and France chose to settle a fortress feud by having a prearranged duel with thirty chosen warriors each. France won the duel and the fort.
10. It is a "lost weapon" whose use had been authenticated in several reliable accounts. It was known to have burned even more rapidly when wet and it could be floated toward enemy ships.

VISUAL QUIZ NUMBER FIVE

MORSE CODE

MORSE CODE

This means of communication is named for its inventor, Samuel F. B. Morse. It is a series of dots, dashes, and spaces that designate an alphabet. In telegraphy the code is transmitted by corresponding sounds.

A	•—
B	—•••
C	•• •
D	—••
E	•
F	•—•
G	——•
H	••••
I	••
J	—•—•
K	—•—
L	⸺
M	——
N	—•
O	• •
P	•••••
Q	••—•
R	• ••
S	•••
T	—
U	••—
V	•••—
W	•——
X	•—••
Y	•• ••
Z	••• •

MORSE CODE

Apply the familiar Morse system to find the names of the following creative finders and inventors. Jot down your answers for the code and the inventor "between the lines" and then turn the page to check them.

1. — •• ——• •••• — —••• ••— — —•••

2. ••••• •••• • • —• •

3. •• • • • — — • • —•   ——• •• —•

4. •—— •• • •• • — • ••• •••

5. ••••• • •— —• ••— —   ••— ••• •

6. • •• •— —•• •• ••— ——   —— • •• •••

7. ••• • •——   • •— •••   •• ••

8. • •• • •— ••••• • • ••

9. ••• — • •— ——

10. ——• •• •• —••   ••• — • • —

MORSE CODE
answers

	CODE	INVENTOR
1.	Lightbulb	Thomas Edison
2.	Phone	Alexander Graham Bell
3.	Cotton gin	Eli Whitney
4.	Wireless	Guglielmo Marconi
5.	Peanut use	George W. Carver
6.	Radium Mrs.	Marie Curie
7.	Sew easy	Elias Howe
8.	Reaper	Cyrus McCormick
9.	Steam	James Watt
10.	Good steel	Henry Bessemer

MUSIC

Ah, there's nothing quite like music to soothe the savage breast or beast. Welcome to an interlude of special fugues and études.

1. One of music's famous "Three B's," he composed his ninth symphony while totally deaf.

2. What band leader directed the Pennsylvanians?

3. Which child prodigy tragically died a pauper at the age of 35?

4. How many keys does a standard piano have?

5. Another of the "Three B's" had a very large musical family. Can you name this family and the number of musicians in it?

6. Which accomplished pianist led a government after one war and led the same nation's government in exile during another world struggle?

7. What are the four movements of a symphony and who is credited with standardizing them?

8. In what type of ballet does each participant and partner combined have a total of six legs?

9. If you knew the answer to question #8, can you explain how a lady named Francesca Caccini is associated with ballet?

10. Which nation defied in 1812 later furnished the music for that defiance?

MUSIC

answers

1. Ludwig van Beethoven.

2. Fred Waring.

3. Wolfgang Amadeus Mozart. He was truly a "universal" composer of such creations as operas, chamber music, symphonies, church music, and both concert and solo pieces for nearly every instrument.

4. The keyboard has 88 keys (36 black and 52 white).

5. The family of Johann Sebastian Bach had 52 such members—give or take a few distant cousins.

6. Ignace Paderewski. He led the Polish government in 1919. Early in World War II, he again was Poland's leader in exile in London.

7. They are the allegro, andante, scherzo, and finale. It was Franz Joseph Haydn, an Austrian composer, who formalized this musical order.

8. The phenomenon occurs in a *ballo à cavallo,* a horse-mounted ballet.

9. In 1625, a Polish prince was visiting the Medici court in Florence, Italy. Francesca Caccini, a court musician, is credited with composing one of the earliest operas in honor of this visit. The lavish spectacle involved horses and developed into a *ballo à cavallo.*

10. England did so, inadvertently. Francis Scott Key's "The Star-Spangled Banner" was written to the tune of a British drinking ditty, "The Anacreontick Song." Thus, in the War of 1812, Key used one of Britain's own songs to glorify the defiance.

MUSIC II

No, this isn't a tape recording. Don't let yourself go flat. Keep your mental notes sharp as you play the following ten "compositions."

1. How was the name of Kay Kaiser's band appropriate to this quiz?
2. What is the most-sung song in English-speaking countries and perhaps even in the Western world?
3. What was unique about Phil Spitalny's band in the Big Band era?
4. What musical implement is common to Antonia Brico, Sarah Caldwell, Victoria Bond, and Judith Somogi?
5. How did the malady known as Marfan's syndrome help Paganini's performance in symphonies?
6. Why are Haydn's *Piano Sonata in A* and Schoenberg's *Pierrot Lunaire* considered musical puzzles?
7. Why is a pianist's right hand in a unique position when playing Chopin's *Étude for Piano in G-flat Major, Opus 10, No. 5?*
8. *Why does John Cage's Imaginary Landscape No. 4* (1953) never sound the same twice when performed live?
9. Why was the South's theme song, "Dixie," the work of an enemy?
10. Should newlyweds look forward to a traditional shivaree beneath their window?

MUSIC II

answers

1. It was called the Kollege of Musical Knowledge.

2. The ever popular "Happy Birthday to You." It was written by Mildred Hill in 1936.

3. Phil's band was the All-Girl Orchestra.

4. The baton. All four women are symphony conductors who had to struggle many years for their well-deserved achievements.

5. Marfan's syndrome is characterized by underdeveloped muscles, very long extremities, and unusually mobile joints. Nicolo Paganini's malady thus enabled him to accomplish unusual effects on the violin through his reach and extension.

6. Haydn's sonata has a minuet with a second section that is identical to the first, except that it is played in reverse. In Schoenberg's work, the music progresses to a halfway point, then follows the opposite pattern, literally "going backward."

7. Chopin's work is also titled the *Black Key Étude.* At only one place does the right hand play a white key.

8. John Cage composed it as a score for twelve randomly tuned radios.

9. It was written by Dan Emmett, an Ohioan and thus a Northerner. He first wrote it in New York for a minstrel "walkaround."

10. Not unless they want to risk embarrassment. A shivaree is a raucous mock serenade with horns, kettles, pans, and other noisemakers.

MYTHOLOGY

According to tales of yore, Greek gods reigned on Olympus and the Norse gods ruled from Asgard. Titans challenged some of these gods, and heroes fought all types of ogres and sorcerers to save fair damsels. Consider the gauntlet of knowledge tossed. Pick it up and you face the maze of questions below. Only the oracles know what monsters may lurk here.

1. The son of Lancelot and Elaine, he was the purest of the Round Table knights and reputedly found the Holy Grail.

2. This Titan stole fire from the gods and gave it to the world.

3. The unicorn is a fabled mythical creature. Can you name the multicultured land of its origin?

4. She was the mistress of Merlin and the Lady of the Lake.

5. He was the chief Germanic god and was associated with the main Norse god, Odin.

6. We've often heard that Adonis was quite a "hunk" in his day. Who was his beautiful, mythic paramour?

7. These three Greek goddesses purveyed charm, elegance, and beauty: Aglaia, Euphrosyne, and Thalia. What were they collectively called?

8. Which monster had a lion's head, a goat's body, and a serpent's tail?

9. Which "sphinx" was fond of telling riddles and how did Oedipus make her a means toward her own end?

10. The ultimate riddle of the Sphinx was: "What walks on four legs at dawn, two legs at midday, and three legs at twilight?" Do you know the answer?

MYTHOLOGY

answers

1. Sir Galahad.

2. Prometheus.

3. The unicorn originated in India.

4. She was Vivian, an enchantress who shared a love of magic with Merlin as well.

5. Woden was his name.

6. Venus was his lover. As the Roman goddess of love, she was "some punkins" herself.

7. The Graces: Aglaia (brilliance), Euphrosyne (joy), and Thalia (bloom).

8. The Chimera, a fire-breathing monster of Greek mythology.

9. The Sphinx at Thebes in Greece. This winged monster with a woman's torso and a lion's trunk perched on a rock near Thebes. Any passer-by who failed to answer a riddle correctly was strangled. Oedipus, a wandering hero, answered a very difficult query and caused the Sphinx to strangle herself.

10. Man. A person crawls on all fours as a baby, walks upright as an adult, and often carries a cane (the third leg) in older years.

MYTHOLOGY II

Are you ready with sword and shield to face yet another onslaught? May the tree trolls bless your safe passage through the following.

1. As the son of Odin, he was the god of thunder and had a magic hammer.

2. When Zeus threw the rebel Titans into Tartarus, why did the Titans go "from the frying pan into the fire"?

3. Though Sinbad had cleared the land and sailed on open seas, he was attacked by rocs. What were they?

4. To the Greeks, this place was the blissful destination of all virtuous people.

5. What wise queen of Carthage used a "little bull" to go a long way?

6. If you see a kelpie in Scotland, why had you better think twice even about taking a bath?

7. Hestia was to the Romans as Vestia was to the Greeks. What did they have in common?

8. What are the mortal but soulless beings who some say still inhabit the air today?

9. Can you name King Arthur's legendary birthplace and his place of burial?

10. What are you supposed to receive if you bend over backwards to kiss the Blarney Stone? Even if you know the answer, why would such acrobatics virtually be impossible?

MYTHOLOGY II

answers

1. He was Thor. The day Thursday is derived from his name.

2. Tartarus was the even more infernal abyss below the pits of Hades.

3. The rocs were giant, man-eating birds.

4. It was Elysium, also known as the Elysian Fields.

5. She was Dido, a Tyrian princess who founded Carthage. She was challenged to secure as much land as she could cover with a bull's hide. Cleverly, she cut the hide in very thin strips and encompassed a larger land mass. This area became the city of Carthage.

6. In Gaelic folklore (Scotland and Ireland included), a kelpie is a water spirit in the form of a horse. It reputedly has the power to warn of a potential drowning or to draw an evil person under any body of water.

7. They were the goddesses of the hearth in both cultures.

8. They are known as sylphs. The German physician and alchemist Paracelsus defined them in his classifications of the world's flora and fauna.

9. He was supposedly born at Tintagel Head, a cape in western Cornwall, England. His burial site was on the island of Avalon, "a paradise in the west" for heroes.

10. You receive "sweet persuasive eloquence," or the gift of blarney. However, the stone is located on the wall of Blarney Castle in County Cork, Ireland. To reach the stone and bend backward too would be quite a feat indeed.

MYTHOLOGY III

From the misty bogs through the forest fogs and across the serpent-filled seas, here are more marvelous myths!

1. They were the king and queen of the Roman gods.
2. Can you name the great hall where Norse heroes' souls were met by Odin after the warriors bravely fell in battle?
3. These chaps were the messengers for the Greek and Roman gods respectively.
4. Who were Calliope, Euterpe, and Thalia?
5. What do the Aramanthean Boar, the Cyrinean Hind, and the Nemean Lion have in common?
6. She was the evil sorceress whose wiles tricked even the powerful Merlin.
7. What on earth does a mythological Greek giant have to do with a peacock (such as the NBC symbol)?
8. Where was the land of Lemuria?
9. Why did Iris, the Greek goddess of the rainbow, need talaria in the *Iliad?*
10. Who were the famous female warriors of ancient lore and where did they supposedly live? *Note:* No half credits are given here. You didn't expect a number 10 question to be easy, did you?

MYTHOLOGY III

answers

1. Jupiter and Juno.

2. Valhalla.

3. Hermes and Mercury.

4. They were three of the nine Muses, the Greek goddesses who presided over literature, the arts, and sciences: Calliope, epic poetry; Euterpe, music; and Thalia, comedy.

5. They were three creatures involved in Hercules' twelve labors as he strove to achieve immortality.

6. She was Morgan le Fay. Some accounts define her as the cruel half sister of King Arthur.

7. The giant was Argus. Zeus gave him a hundred eyes to watch Zeus's secret love, the maiden Io. For his loyalty, Zeus made Argus's eyes immortal by placing them in the peacock's tail.

8. Lemuria is believed by some to be a "lost land" in the current-day Indian Ocean. There lemurlike primates once lived. German biologist Ernst Haeckel proposed this hypothesis.

9. Talaria were the winged sandals worn by messengers. In Homer's *Iliad,* Iris was the gods' messenger.

10. They were the Amazons. They lived in Scythia, a kingdom believed to be near the Black Sea.

NURSERY RHYMES AND TALES

We think we've outgrown cute little nursery rhymes until we see someone on a quiz show who wins big bucks by knowing one. Search your early memories for answers about these stories and verses.

1. In "Jack and the Beanstalk," what did Jack get in exchange for his cow?
2. Who caused a panic in the barnyard with tales that the sky was falling?
3. Who had to sing for his supper? By the way, what was his supper?
4. In the story "The Ugly Duckling," what was the duckling?
5. What were the materials that the three pigs used to protect themselves from the wolf?
6. When King Cole called for a few things, what was the total number he received in response?
7. In "Sing a Song of Sixpence," how many blackbirds were baked in the pie?
8. For one a penny, two a penny, what could you buy?
9. At what hour did Wee Willy Winkie run upstairs and downstairs? How was he attired?
10. Where did one go to meet the woman with rings on her fingers and bells on her toes?

NURSERY RHYMES AND TALES

answers

1. He got magic beans.
2. Chicken Little.
3. Tommy Tucker. His supper was white bread and butter.
4. Actually, it was a beautiful swan.
5. They used twigs, straw, and bricks in that order.
6. Five was the total, including his pipe, his bowl, and the fiddlers three.
7. Twenty-four (or four-and-twenty, as the rhyme says).
8. You could buy hot cross buns.
9. He did his galavanting at eight o'clock in his nightgown.
10. One went to Banbury Cross.

ODDITIES

The word odd means out of the ordinary, unusual, peculiar, singular. Well, you'll certainly find this collection fits that definition like the proverbial glove.

1. She was Howdy Doody's sister. *Clue:* In a famous children's book, a girl with the same first name often heard yodelers.
2. What does legerdemain have to do with hats, cards, and puffs of smoke?
3. Can you name the TV dog that wears a trenchcoat and "takes a bite out of crime"?
4. He was the little-known Sherpa guide who reached Mt. Everest's peak with Edmund Hillary in 1953.
5. Why is a koan such a puzzle to students of Zen Buddhism?
6. What would you be doing if you were belaying your nuts?
7. Though he accomplished little during his rule, Napoleon III of France left the world one fashion of an "imperial" nature. Can you describe it?
8. What are you seeing if you look at a Mercator projection?
9. Why was Helicon quite unlike Hades to the Greeks?
10. What do the letters IOOF stand for?

ODDITIES

answers

1. She was Heidi Doody. (However, she took a back seat in the Peanut Gallery to the show's real "looker," Princess Summer-Fall-Winter-Spring.)

2. It means sleight of hand, another name for a magician's tricks.

3. He is McGruff.

4. He was Tenzing Norkay and played a key role in the conquest of Everest.

5. A koan is a riddle used to test and teach Zen acolytes.

6. You'd be mountain climbing. Belaying involves moving and anchoring the ropes. Nuts are the wedges a climber drives into the rocks.

7. It was the "imperial" beard. Louis Napoleon wore a modified goatee with a small, pointed tuft of beard on his lower lip and chin.

8. A map of the earth in rectangular form that provides some varied perspectives on geography and other features.

9. There were two main reasons. Helicon was supposedly on mountainous heights in southern Greece. Furthermore, it was the reputed home of the Muses, in whose company any mortal should have been quite overjoyed.

10. The Independent Order of Odd Fellows, a benevolent secret society founded in England in the eighteenth century.

OLYMPICS (SUMMER AND WINTER)

Though the Olympics are plagued by politics and questions of amateur status, they remain the world's most colossal competition.

1. What nation originated the first Olympiad and renewed the modern-day Olympics?
2. Which hockey match is considered perhaps the greatest upset in all of amateur or professional sports?
3. Who had America's only major swimming success in the 1932 Olympics at Los Angeles? *Clue:* He later was the movies' Flash Gordon.
4. Who won an unprecedented five individual gold medals in skating?
5. She was an outstanding all-around athlete who won two gold medals in the 1932 Olympics.
6. This track star was nicknamed the Flying Finn.
7. Who dazzled the judges and all competitors with her skating in the 1930s? What was her native land?
8. Who is the only person to win gold medals in both the winter and summer games?
9. What do the Olympic colored rings symbolize?
10. The Olympic motto is "Citius, altius, fortius." Can you translate it?

OLYMPICS (SUMMER AND WINTER)

answers

1. Greece. Olympiados was a district of ancient Elis where the games and festivals in honor of Zeus were first held. The modern competitions were renewed in Athens in 1896.

2. The U.S. hockey team's victory over the Soviet Union in the 1980 Olympics at Lake Placid, New York. This devastating upset of the highly trained Russians enabled the American team to go on to win the gold medal.

3. Buster Crabbe. His achievement enabled him to secure movie roles that matched his 1932 heroism.

4. Eric Heiden, a speed skater, accomplished this remarkable record at the 1980 games in Lake Placid. He won the following meter races: 500, 1,000, 1,500, 5,000, and 10,000.

5. Mildred "Babe" Didrickson was one of America's all-time great athletes. In 1932 Olympic rules limited her to entering only three events. She won in both the javelin and the 80-meter hurdles. Judges denied her the gold in the high jump because of her head-first style. Undaunted, she went on to achieve top successes in a number of sports.

6. He was Paavo Nurmi. This Finnish star won nine gold medals in track in the Olympic games held during the 1920s and early 1930s.

7. Her name was Sonja Henie. A Norwegian, she applied her athletic ability to a film career.

8. American Eddie Eagan accomplished this very rare feat. In 1920 in Antwerp, Belgium, he won the boxing gold in the light-heavyweight division. In 1932 at Lake Placid, he was on the winning U.S. four-man bobsled team.

9. The five rings symbolize the five major continents. The colors are green, yellow, black, blue, and red. At least one of them is found on the national banner of every country.

10. It means "Faster, higher, stronger."

OPERA

Though opera has existed for centuries, it has not always enjoyed widespread public recognition. As opera increases in popularity, it is becoming an area rich in unusual facts.

1. Her nickname is "Bubbles" and she often speaks on TV about opera's many facets.
2. Whose operettas have remained popular since they were first performed at England's Savoy Theatre?
3. Which tragic heroine was stabbed by Don Jose and in what opera did this occur?
4. Can you translate the title of Johann Stauss's opera *Der Fledermaus? Clue*: The title has much in common with a mammal associated with vampire stories.
5. What are the two tasty food items named for the Australian prima donna Helen Mitchell Armstrong?
6. In which opera are the Dukes of Mantua and Galatea prime characters?
7. Can you name the opera by Donizetti known for its nine high C's?
8. What was Beethoven's only opera?
9. What character in *The Magic Flute* plays the title instrument to protect himself?
10. To grab the gold ring for this section, please name the operas in the Nibelungen Cycle.

OPERA

answers

1. She is Beverly Sills and she has done much to bring an appreciation of opera to the world.

2. They are the creations of Sir William Gilbert and Sir Arthur Sullivan.

3. *Carmen* is the name of the opera and its heroine.

4. It means *The Bat*.

5. Mrs. Armstrong is better known as Dame Nellie Melba. The taste tempters are Melba toast and peach Melba.

6. They are characters in *Rigoletto* by Verdi.

7. It is *The Daughter of the Regiment.*

8. It is *Fidelio*.

9. He is Prince Tamino in the opera by Mozart.

10. These inspiring achievements by Wagner are *Das Rheingold, Die Walkure, Siegfried,* and *Die Götterdämmerung*.

PASTIMES

Here is another collection of the many ways in which we *passe-temps*. That's the French way of saying the above title. Enough time spent talking.

1. Some of its varieties are shotgun, cutthroat, and three-card monte.
2. In this game, you have to start with 90 feet before you can even try to score.
3. This board competition has 24 spear-shaped divisions.
4. Which game has double-letter and triple-work scores?
5. In which card contest do players bet on the cards to be turned up from the top of the dealer's deck?
6. You've heard about real and mistaken "domino theories" in politics, but do you know how many dots are on a domino?
7. In what kind of competition would you find the popping crease?
8. Define the interesting pieces and the special board design of the game that could be called "Far East draughts."
9. What is a chukker?
10. Why does Joan Pope, known to the French as the Yellow Dwarf, have any reason to be mentioned here?

PASTIMES

answers

1. Poker is the game.

2. It is baseball. There are 90 feet between home plate and first base.

3. It is backgammon and the divisions are called points.

4. The game is Scrabble.

5. The contest is faro. It reputedly gained its name from the image of an Egyptian king on the back of one of the cards.

6. Each face of a domino tile is divided in half. In either half there can be as few as one or as many as six dots. Therefore, on the whole domino's side, there can be as few as two or as many as twelve dots.

7. In a cricket match. It is a line marking the batter's position.

8. "Far East draughts" is better known as Chinese checkers. The pieces are marbles and the board has a six-pointed star with holes for the marbles.

9. It is a period of time in polo lasting 7½ minutes.

10. Joan Pope and Yellow Dwarf are names for the same card game. In it there are no set number of players and the eight of diamonds is removed from the deck.

PASTIMES II

Now you know what *passe-temps* means. Will you be able to say the same for the following?

1. If you raised Jacob's ladder to look for the witch's hat, what would you be doing?

2. Can you name the two letters that are both worth 10 points in Scrabble?

3. What is the name of the three-cornered board with a pencil that writes messages?

4. When would you use a Benoni, a Queen's Indian, and a Caro-Kann?

5. Normally, in an official skeet match, from how many angles must you shoot?

6. This card game is played like dominoes, the object being to match exposed cards to win.

7. In 1938, in various parts of California, an auto competition called Motor Roto was held. Please describe it.

8. In the card game seven-up, why would Pedro's presence be fortuitous?

9. Can you name the poles that the Scots "toss" in their clan games?

10. Both military collectors and military brass place miniatures on strategy boards. Whether as a hobby or for real, what is this called?

PASTIMES II

answers

1. They are games similar to cat's cradle and are played with string.

2. The letters Q and Z.

3. It is a planchette.

4. In a chess match. They are types of defenses.

5. Eight angles are required.

6. It is muggins. Its name derives from a British term for a card sharper's dupe.

7. It was a demolition-derby-type competition in which cars tried to move a giant ball across a playing field and over their opponents' "goal line."

8. Seven-up has two to four players, and seven points wins the game. Pedro is a variation of it, in which Pedro, as a trump card, counts five points.

9. They are called cabers. Some of them weigh over 60 pounds.

10. Kriegspiel (German: *krieg,* war + *spiel*, game). In a formal sense, it is a means of teaching war strategy on a map representing terrain.

PHOBIAS

Whether it's a slimy, creepie-crawlie, or a dark, foggy night, most of us have at least one fear that either makes us want to cringe or causes our knees to feel like quivering jelly. Brace yourself as you match the phobia with its fear.

1. Acrophobia: (a) strangers (b) being alone (c) heights

2. Claustrophobia: (a) blood (b) enclosures (c) animals

3. Zoophobia: (a) strangers (b) animals (c) prisons

4. Monophobia: (a) money (b) blood (c) being alone

5. Nucleomitiphobia: (a) strangers (b) depth (c) nuclear bombs

6. Xenophobia: (a) strangers (b) disease (c) open spaces

7. Chromophobia: (a) chrome (b) blood (c) certain colors

8. Domatophobia: (a) being dominated (b) depth (c) confinement

9. Pathophobia: (a) insects (b) disease (c) fear of fear

10. Mysophobia: (a) germs (b) making decisions (c) fame

PHOBIAS
answers

1. (c) heights
2. (b) enclosures
3. (b) animals
4. (c) being alone
5. (c) nuclear bombs
6. (a) strangers
7. (c) certain colors
8. (c) confinement
9. (b) disease
10. (a) germs

PHOBIAS II

Here's another chance to be thankful that you don't have any of these phobias. To avoid them, don't walk along any steep ledges, enter wide open spaces, eat strange food, touch door knobs, or go to bed without a nightlight, etc. Yes, they seem as endless as one's imagination. Yet, one's mind can control each and all of them.

1. Androphobia: (a) animals (b) men (c) poverty
2. Baccilophobia: (a) bridges (b) microbes (c) pain
3. Gynephobia: (a) gymnasiums (b) nakedness (c) women
4. Bathophobia: (a) water (b) depth (c) showers
5. Aerophobia: (a) fog (b) airplanes (c) high objects
6. Astrophobia: (a) storms (b) stars (c) horoscopes
7. Ergophobia: (a) being wrong (b) work (c) fame
8. Gephydrophobia (a) water (b) fish (c) crossing bridges
9. Algophobia: (a) doctors (b) pain (c) dentists
10. Pantophobia: (a) fear of fear (b) zippers (c) breathlessness

Bonus: To gain a chance for redemption, define the very real fear with the very real spelling Arachibutyrophobia.

PHOBIAS II

answers

1. (b) men
2. (b) microbes
3. (c) women
4. (b) depth
5. (c) high objects
6. (a) storms
7. (b) work
8. (c) crossing bridges
9. (b) pain
10. (a) fear of fear

Bonus: Arachibutyrophobia is the fear of having peanut butter stick to the roof of one's mouth, thus causing choking and various other misfortunes.

PHOTOGRAPHY

It is an age-old saying that a picture is worth a thousand words and then some. Yet we often think of pictures in particular and of photography in general as recent means of recording events. Actually, photography has a detailed and fascinating past, as we shall now see.

1. He was the photographer whose bravery and foresight enabled him to record the U.S. Civil War.

2. Simply, what does the word Kodak mean?

3. Who created the special process we know today as Polaroid?

4. In 1490 Leonardo da Vinci described the camera obscura. What is it and how is it used today?

5. Do you know who took the world's "first photograph" and when it was taken?

6. Created in 1837, this process made use of a silvered copperplate sensitized with a base of iodine. It produces a positive without a negative and was popular until the 1860s.

7. To an early photographer, what were trade ticklers?

8. Pinups became quite popular in the 1940s. Previously, they were named for a specific part of the anatomy. Can you give the pinup's other name?

9. To which branch of the U.S. armed services was a photographer assigned in World War I?

10. How did the Airgraph, also known as V-Mail, lead to both improved information storage and more devious spying?

PHOTOGRAPHY

answers

1. He was Matthew B. Brady.

2. It has no meaning whatsoever. George Eastman, the founder of Kodak, created the word for that very reason (it was unlike any other).

3. Edwin Herbert Land accomplished this after discovering the process in the early 1930s.

4. The camera obscura (Latin: dark chamber) is a box for sketching objects. The box has a mirror and a double-convex lens at the front end. An image is reflected upon a glass screen at the top of the box where it can be sketched. Today it is used in exhibits of camera history.

5. It was taken by Frenchman Joseph Niépce in 1826. He experimented with pewter plates treated with bitumen of Judea and oil of lavender. From his workroom window, he exposed the plate over eight hours on a summer day.

6. It was the daguerreotype, named after its inventor, Louis J. M. Daguerre, a French artist.

7. They were showcase cards that described a photo studio's services. They were also known as trade pullers, attracting business in the early 1900s.

8. Portrait photographers once called them "leg art." In World War II, the badly painted walls of many large military bases were natural sites for a pinup's welcome visual relief.

9. In the early months of the war, many photographers entered the Army Signal Corps. Eventually, with the expansion of aerial photo needs, they expanded into all the service branches.

10. Kodak's Airgraph was a mailing program begun in World War II. Letters between home and the front were reduced on an early form of microfilm. Overseas, the film images were enlarged. Thus, microfilm's progress was greatly enhanced—as was the spying trade.

PHOTOGRAPHY (OTHER DEVELOPMENTS)

From the days of wet plates to today's laser-defined pictures, photography has come a long way. Here are some other examples.

1. Define the difference between a ferrotype and a tintype.
2. Which U.S. President credited photos with changing his gangling, awkward image to one of a mature man? *Clue*: He said it helped him win his biggest election.
3. In the early 1900s what were Aristo proofs?
4. Why did the humerus and the nape play such an important role in early photo studios?
5. By the mid-1930s, magazines and movies brought this type of photographer-facts gatherer into vogue.
6. Why was a Rochester, New York, building "bombed" to prove a point about aerial photos?
7. Remember the camera obscura? What relation, if any, does the camera lucida have to it?
8. Can you define the difference between photoengraving and photogravure?
9. What devastating but infrequently mentioned fire was the subject of the world's first news photo?
10. After all these definitions, do you have a better idea of what a camerlengo is?

PHOTOGRAPHY (OTHER DEVELOPMENTS)

answers

1. They are the same type of photo. Both are positive photos taken directly on a plate that is coated with a sensitized form of film. The plates can be made of thin iron (ferrotype) or tin (tintype).
2. He was Abraham Lincoln. Some of his political rivals tried to portray him as a naïve hayseed. However, his friends circulated his photos, which quite capably showed his true self.
3. In 1900 the American Aristotype Company, a producer of photo products encouraged photographers to advertise their creations as potential Christmas presents. Cards with family photos were the "proofs."
4. The sun's proper exposure and the subject's position had to be carefully balanced. Therefore, arm rests and neck clamps became necessary to help a person hold his or her position.
5. The photojournalist. This intrepid reporter-photographer continues to get into and out of jams by exposing crime and corruption.
6. General Geoge Goddard "flash bombed" Rochester's Kodak Tower on November 20, 1925. He used 90 pounds of photo flash powder in a successful test of aerial reconnaissance at night.
7. The camera lucida (Latin: light chamber) is also a device used for sketching. It consists of a frame support, a four-sided prism, and a magnifying glass. The prism is placed at an angle and reflects the image toward a glass sheet where the sketch is made.
8. In photoengraving, photographs are made from plates that have the reproduction in relief. In photogravure, photos are reproduced on intaglio (engraved) plates or on rolls that have a satinlike finish.
9. It was the fire that raged through Hamburg, Germany, from May 5 to May 8, 1842. Using the daguerreotype process, German photographers Hermann Biow and Carl Stelzner recorded the disaster for posterity.
10. A camerlengo has nothing to do with a camera (except in the Latin sense of "chamber"). He is a cardinal in charge of the Vatican's treasury.

POLITICS

Politics has been called "the art of the possible." It also has been called—well, you can imagine. Now, let's enter the reality of the hustings as we begin the chicken-and-green-peas circuit.

1. They were an early American party whose name sounded very much like a hairpiece.

2. In 1912, which group was led by "Bully" Roosevelt and had the largest member of the deer family as its symbol.

3. Some say both overconfidence and a wedding cake's groom led to this man's defeat.

4. This group's name is associated with forward movement. It has had an effect on politics during several periods with similar party names and goals.

5. Who was the golden-voiced orator whose silver issues weren't enough to help him achieve the presidency?

6. The name of this "boss" sounds like a type of clothing material. He fleeced the shirts from many before his fall.

7. Members of this party said that they had no knowledge about their own secret coalition. In the 1800s, they tried to elect only native-born Protestant Americans.

8. These reformers within a major party chose their name from the Algonquian word for "great man" or "chief." Later, the name became associated with independents everywhere.

9. This "anti" organization held the first presidential nominating convention. It chose a most ironic candidate.

10. Though its "work" was limited, this was the first labor-oriented party in the United States and perhaps the entire world.

POLITICS

answers

1. They were the Whigs. From 1836 to 1856, they were the main opposition to the Democrats. The Whigs favored industrial protection and limits upon the President's powers.

2. They were the Bull Moose party and were a combination of former Populists and reformers, among others.

3. He was Thomas E. Dewey. Though considered the frontrunner, Republican Dewey lost to Harry Truman. A Truman supporter, Alice Roosevelt Longworth compared Dewey to a wedding cake's groom. Some experts do believe this swayed some "undecideds" away from Dewey.

4. The Progressive party. Also called the National Progressive party, its coalitions have been led by Teddy Roosevelt (1912), Robert LaFollette (1924), and Henry A. Wallace (1948).

5. William Jennings Bryan favored free coinage of silver and agrarian reform but failed in three presidential bids.

6. He was William M. Tweed, who "bossed" the corrupt Tammany Hall political machine. Tweed and his group misappropriated millions from New York City between 1868 and 1871.

7. The Know-Nothing party was known for its secretive ways from 1853 to 1856. It was a coalition of anti-Catholic, anti-immigrant groups.

8. The Mugwumps (Algonquian: *mugquomp*, chief). They were Republican party reformers who refused to support the 1884 presidential ticket.

9. The Anti-Mason party. In September of 1831, its members gathered in Baltimore, Maryland. Strangely, through various political tradeoffs, they chose William Wirt, a loyal Mason. (In 1832, Wirt carried only Vermont.)

10. It was the Working Man's party. Originating in New York and Philadelphia, it existed from 1828 to 1830, promoting a platform of a ten-hour day, an end to debtors' prisons, and more public schools.

POTPOURRI

Potpourri (Spanish: *olla-podrida*, a stew) can be a medley, an anthology, or a miscellany. As with any really good stew, there's a bit o' everythin' in it for you.

1. What did the earth's reputedly first man, an English genius, a Swiss archer, and an American wilderness wanderer have in common?

2. This item of apparel—variously labeled a call, compromise, and go-between coat—was named after a country club in New York.

3. In the popular children's story, which animal preferred smelling the flowers to fighting?

4. Why might you expect to find horses of the pommel variety in a turnverein?

5. What is a zamboni and why is it always involved in a "scrape"?

6. The statue of freedom might be another name for the Statue of Liberty. But can you name the location of the real Statue of Freedom?

7. What was the "right of clergy" exercised in the Middle Ages?

8. Yes, there is another kind of unicorn—the sea unicorn. What is it?

9. Many coins have approximately a hundred of the seemingly useless things called knurls. What are they?

10. Who in the world was Hermes Trismegistus and what does he have to do with Johnny Carson's character Carnac on *The Tonight Show*?

POTPOURRI

answers

1. They had the apple in common. In the Bible, Adam ate it. An apple reputedly inspired Sir Isaac Newton. William Tell shot one from atop his son's head. Johnny Appleseed planted seeds across the Midwest.

2. It was the tuxedo. The country club was Tuxedo Park in Tuxedo Lake, New York.

3. He was Ferdinand the Bull and he preferred gardens to the bull ring.

4. A turnverein (Greek: *turnen,* to exercise + *verein*, a club) is a gymnast's club.

5. It is an ice-clearing vehicle seen at hockey arenas or ice rinks. It "scrapes" the surface clean. The Zamboni company builds them.

6. The Statue of Freedom is located atop the Capitol Building in Washington, D.C.

7. In those troubled days of "confused justice," if you could read and in some cases write, you could avoid hanging offenses. Few besides the educated clergy could either read or write. Therefore, anyone else who could do so had an advantage.

8. It is the narwhal. This Arctic cetacean is sought for its ivory and oil. The spiral tusk of the male, which extends from its upper jaw, creates the unicorn similarity.

9. Knurls are the ridges on the edges.

10. Hermes Trismegistus ("Hermes the thrice greatest") was the Greek name for Thoth, the Egyptian god of alchemy and the occult. The word *hermetic*, or airtight, derives from this. Carnac, the all-wise sage, keeps his answers in a hermetically sealed jar on Funk and Wagnall's porch.

QUARKS 'N' QUIRKS

Herein you will find a collection of questions from the realm of science in general and such areas as the stars, inventiveness, and the weather in particular. However, don't assume anything about anything . . .

1. What is the more common name for the breathing aid known as the drinker respirator?

2. Which Austrian physicist has had his name applied to speed measurements?

3. Who was the man who didn't take a shower but who did become known as the Father of Experimental Science?

4. What on, or around, the earth is a spelunker?

5. Which scientist is credited with developing electricity through chemical means?

6. Who or what can be measured by the Beaufort scale?

7. Where might one locate his or her lunulas?

8. What is the name of the weather map that encompasses the conditions of a region for a given period of time?

9. Using the moon as an example, define its apogee and perigee in relation to the earth.

10. What does a German word for a sour-milk product have to do with subatomic particles and this category?

QUARKS 'N' QUIRKS

answers

1. The Iron Lung. American inventor Philip Drinker created the life-saving device.

2. He was Ernst Mach. The Mach number concerns the ratio of an object's air speed to the speed of sound in the same atmospheric region.

3. He was Archimedes, a Greek physicist. Reputedly, while taking a bath, he discovered the key principle of specific gravity as it related to displacement of the water by his body.

4. A spelunker is a person who practices speleology, the science of exploring caves.

5. He was Luigi Galvani, an Italian physiologist and physicist. He experimented with batteries to produce electric current.

6. The Beaufort scale, developed by British naval officer Sir Francis Beaufort, is used to measure wind velocity. The scale ranges from 0 (for speeds less than 1 mile per hour) to 12 (for 72 miles per hour). The former would be a calm. The latter is hurricane force.

7. Lunulas are the whitish, half-moon shapes at the base of the fingernails.

8. It is a synoptic chart (Latin: *synopticus*, a summary).

9. The moon's apogee is its orbiting point farthest from the earth. Its perigee is its orbiting point nearest to the earth.

10. The word is *quark*. It is the German for cottage cheese (sour-milk curds). It also is the English word for a new and unique series of subatomic particles. Quarks may have the tiniest known electrical charges and may be the basis of all matter.

QUARKS 'N' MORE QUIRKS

Yes, you know what a quark is now. Of course, inquisitive person that you are, you probably knew the answer already. But hold your hydrogen atoms. Science is chock full o' quirks by the score. Surely, wise one that you are, you must have known that there would be more.

1. What is the better-known name for Hanson's disease, the affliction that led to the creation of "colonies"?

2. Which aristocratic family is listed in that blue blooded compilation of elements, the periodic table?

3. What is the more common term for a vasovagal response? *Clue*: It has been referred to as everything from "spells" to "wim-wams."

4. Can you name the critical constants?

5. Is Willis's Circle a subject near the realm of the human mind, or is it an orb of the heavens?

6. What was the first "long distance" scientific weapon of war?

7. Name the North Star, describe why the name is so chosen, and define its constellation.

8. When a comet is moving away from the sun, its tail is pointing _____. However, when a comet approaches the sun, the tail points _____. Explain both answers.

9. The ancient Egyptians practiced a ritual related to astronomy that generally deciphers as "birth of the sun's cane." Please define this in lay terms.

10. Which ten-tentacled cephalopod's name is an acronym for an instrument used to measure fields of magnetism? By the way, what is the device's full name?

QUARKS 'N' MORE QUIRKS

answers

1. It is leprosy. Arn Hansen was the Norwegian doctor who discovered the bacterium that caused leprosy.

2. The "aristocrats" are the noble gases, which include: argon, helium, krypton, neon, radon, and xenon.

3. It is a fainting spell. The vaso (vessel) part occurs when veins dilate and trap blood. Less blood reaches the brain and one gets dizzy and can fall. The vagal aspect concerns the vagus nerve. When a person falls, the vagus nerve signals the heart to beat more slowly. The body is recumbent and the blood circulates more easily. The brain is nourished sufficiently and consciousness returns.

4. They are the temperature, pressure, density, and volume of a substance.

5. It is quite near the mind. In fact, it is the arterial circle at the brain's base. An English doctor, Thomas Willis, discovered it.

6. The telescope. In 1608, the Netherlands and Spain were at war. The Dutch used their invention to watch the Spanish ships. By noting the Spaniards' intended directions and fleet size on several occasions, the Dutch made the telescope a spy's weapon and thus a weapon of war when they counterattacked.

7. Polaris is the North Star because it is the star most visibly close to true north. It is located in the tail of the constellation called the Little Bear.

8. *Away* is the answer for both. The sun's wind causes a comet's dust particles to be formed into a tail. This solar wind is made up of subatomic particles that have this effect whatever a comet's direction.

9. The Egyptians performed a ritual during the autumnal equinox. They believed that the sun was faltering and needed a cane or staff for support.

10. It is a squid. Its name is an acronym for *s*uperconductive *qu*antum *i*nterference *d*evice. This instrument is currently the best for measuring magnetic fields.

QUESTS

Don your sword and buckler. Keep that fair maiden's scarf safely tucked away as you ride out on your trusty steed or take the wheel of your sleek frigate. Brace yourself for adventure as you join other seekers on courses charted for untold power and glory!

1. Which spiritually significant chalice was the objective of many medieval journeys?
2. Regarding #1, what do *Parsifal, Morte d'Arthur,* and *Idylls of the King* have in common?
3. This was the much-sought-after gateway through the Americas to the Orient's wonders.
4. Can you name the first person to fly over both poles?
5. Who was Passepartout and what on earth did he do?
6. How did a saint, a horse, and a little girl combine to make world-changing discoveries?
7. Who were the duo Cipango and Cathay, and what did they mean to the early navigator-explorers?
8. Who was the Shoshoni Indian woman responsible for guiding William and Meriwether on their trek?
9. Why should the name Juan Sebastian del Cano be listed with the world's great navigators?
10. Why did Nelly Bly not exactly go around the world in 1890 in 72 days?

QUESTS

answers

1. It was the Holy Grail. In legend, it was considered to be either the cup or the platter used by Jesus at the Last Supper. The Grail disappeared due to the impure lives of its keepers.

2. They each are associated with the search for the Holy Grail. *Parsifal* is a Wagner opera. Mallory's *Morte d'Arthur* and Tennyson's *Idylls of the King* are stories involved in part wih the Round Table knights' search for the Grail.

3. It was the Northwest Passage. Eventually, the passage was found as a waterway through the islands and coastal waters of North America.

4. He was U.S. Admiral Richard E. Byrd.

5. He was the valet of Phileas Fogg. Together they made the epic, fictional 80-day journey around the world.

6. The saint was the *Santa Maria*. The horse was the *Pinta*, and the girl was the *Niña*. Of course, they were Colombus's vessels during his historic voyage.

7. They were Japan and China to Occidental Europeans. They were the lands of treasure sought by many. Marco Polo is credited with giving Japan the name Cipango.

8. She was Sacajawea and she contributed much to the success of the Clark and Lewis expedition.

9. He was Magellan's navigator. When Magellan was killed in the Philippines, Cano assumed command of Magellan's *Victoria* and completed the voyage around the globe.

10. Nelly Bly only circled the earth as the pseudonym of Elizabeth Seaman, an ambitious New York journalist.

QUIZ AND GAME SHOWS

From the early days of radio to the technical marvels of television, quiz and game shows have been with us. They have both informed us and left us wondering about some of the apparent answers. Below you will find questions about these very shows and their hosts.

1. In this game show, if you did not answer correctly, you suffered a "punishment" of often hilarious proportions. *Clue:* It is also the name of a New Mexico town.

2. On this 1950s and 1960s program, a lucky lady got to have a "day."

3. A famous comedian in his own right, he was the host of *Laugh Line*.

4. The object of this 1960s game, which was emceed by Tom Kennedy, was to say only so much.

5. Can you name the two shows that tested musical knowledge and were hosted by Bert Parks and George DeWitt?

6. Hostess of *Just Men*, she has been a TV and quiz-show regular.

7. Which program required the panelists to describe various objects, inventions, etc., in unusually persuasive and creative ways?

8. This show from TV's "golden age" was hosted by Ernie Kovaks and sometimes required trifocals.

9. *Stump the Stars* was a type of charades or pantomime quiz. Can you name its emcee?

10. What was the first nationally televised program of a quiz or question nature?

QUIZ AND GAME SHOWS

answers

1. It was *Truth or Consequences* and was hosted by Ralph Edwards.

2. This show was *Queen for a Day* with Jack Baily.

3. He is Dick Van Dyke.

4. It was called *You Don't Say.*

5. *Name That Tune* was hosted by George DeWitt originally. *Stop the Music* had Bert Parks for its emcee.

6. She is Betty White and she has been one of the few women to be a hostess of such programs.

7. It was the *Liars' Club*, hosted by Allen Ludden.

8. *Take a Good Look* was a show that required very careful watching in the 1950s.

9. He was Mike Stokey and he maintained decorum amid some of the stars' wild antics.

10. It was the 1939 National Spelling Bee. At that time, radio was the quiz-show haven and TV was still in its early days when a few fortunate viewers saw this broadcast on the East Coast.

QUIZ WHIZ

The following "stumpers" have been collected from those ubiquitous repositories of knowledge—TV game shows. If you had just five seconds and yet another vacation to Inner Mongolia was on the line, could you correctly answer these?

1. Who were the little folks Gulliver met on his travels?
2. What is the name of the game in which polished stones are pushed toward tees 38 yards apart on an icy surface?
3. What portmanteau word names the condition of the air around Los Angeles?
4. If you were having auditory difficulties because of too much cerumen, what would be your problem?
5. If you have been given your mittimus, what have you lost?
6. Who was the "last" Mohican?
7. When you roll "boxcars" in dice, what do you have?
8. What basic math problem of circles and squares is considered currently impossible to solve?
9. Why might one get a "bang" out of being hoisted on his/her own petard?
10. When may any stone be said to be "living"?

QUIZ WHIZ

answers

1. They were the Lilliputians.

2. It is curling. This name derives from the curling angle in which the stones sometimes move. The Scottish name for a curling match is a bonspiel.

3. Smog is the word. Portmanteau words are combinations of two other words that are very similar in spelling and definition. For example, fog + smoke = smog.

4. You would have an overabundance of ear wax.

5. You've lost your job—since it means getting fired. It is also a warrant for placing a convicted person in jail.

6. He was Uncas of the James Fenimore Cooper epic.

7. You have two 6's.

8. The squaring of a circle remains unsolvable within present mathematical means.

9. A petard was a medieval explosive device. It consisted of a metal cone filled with powder and attached to an enemy's wall, gate, etc. In *Hamlet*, the petard hoisting involved being destroyed by the very means meant to ruin others.

10. When a sculptor creates a figure of stone and leaves it in its natural surroundings, it is said to be "living stone."

RADIO (FROM TUBES TO TRANSISTORS)

Only the Shadow knew the real secret of the *Inner Sanctum*. But even that great "shade" didn't know all of the answers below. Do you? Woe unto those who fail! A-ha-ha-haaaaa!

1. On this show you often heard the question, "Pa, who in tarnation was that masked man?"
2. His show was *The Original Amateur Hour.*
3. Her name was Molly and her husband had a famous cupboard. Who was he?
4. She was Baby Snooks for some 14 years.
5. Which girl from a "western mining town" tried to find happiness with a titled Englishman?
6. What was the complete name of the Great Gildersleeve?
7. Who actually was *The Falcon*'s other self?
8. Can you name Ma Perkins's daughters?
9. Who were Billy Jones and Ernie Hare?
10. Define Conelrad and locate it on the dial.

RADIO (FROM TUBES TO TRANSISTORS)

answers

1. The masked man was *The Lone Ranger*.

2. He was Major Bowes.

3. He was Fibber McGee. He and Molly lived at 79 Wistful Vista.

4. Fanny Brice, a great comedienne, had this role.

5. *Our Gal Sunday* was the lady on this quest.

6. He was Throckmorton P. Gildersleeve.

7. Mike Waring was *The Falcon.*

8. Ma's daughters were Fay and Evey.

9. They were the "Interwoven Pair" of socks from a popular commercial.

10. Conelrad was an acronym for *con*trol of *el*ectromagnetic *rad*iation. It was a Civil Defense warning system that was found on 640 and 1240 AM.

RADIO (THE DIAL TURNS)

Listen with keen anticipation as the dial's pointer passes the static-filled spaces to seek even more audio chills and thrills.

1. During World War II, he was a London broadcaster for the CBS network.
2. This popular show about a schoolteacher was on the air almost 10 years.
3. *Big Town* was a series about what kind of curious careerman?
4. Can you name Jack Benny's car?
5. Which series defined itself as being dedicated to the "Women of America"?
6. For many years, he was the definitive Dagwood.
7. Who was Sam Spade's secretary?
8. Which comic strip became the first children's serial?
9. Which bandleader was nicknamed "poet of the piano"?
10. This NBC music program began in 1928 and continued for 26 years.

RADIO (THE DIAL TURNS)

answers

1. Edward R. Murrow quite capably described the real dangers of war to a still very isolated and vulnerable America.
2. That popular teacher was *Our Miss Brooks*.
3. A newspaperman who wrote the headlines.
4. It was a 1929 Maxwell.
5. *Hilltop House* claimed this distinction.
6. He was Arthur Lake.
7. Effie Perine was the good-natured gal Friday for the hard-boiled crime-buster.
8. Leapin' lizards! It was *Little Orphan Annie.*
9. Carmen Cavallaro was the keyboard poet.
10. The program was *The Voice of Firestone.*

RADIO (ANOTHER STATION)

Oh wow, you've found your favorite show. It's stormy outside, but you're comfy in the mohair armchair; your mug of hot cocoa is steamy warm and you're ready to tackle any foe or answer any question!

1. On the *Amos 'n' Andy Show*, what was Amos's last name?
2. Who had the *Flight of the Bumblebee* for a theme?
3. What was the first commercially successful radio station in the U.S.?
4. In which city did *Pepper Young's Family* live?
5. What was Marge's relationship with Myrt?
6. Can you name Corliss Archer's boyfriend?
7. What bandleader used strange sound effects to make humorous variations in popular songs? Can you identify his group?
8. Who offered to pay anyone who could prove that he tricked people with his mind-reading act?
9. On which show did a squeaking door often affect the air time? What was the significance of this?
10. What was *The Shadow*'s name and who was the one person in the world who knew his identity?

RADIO (ANOTHER STATION)

answers

1. He was Amos Jones.

2. It was the *Green Hornet*'s song.

3. It was KDKA in Pittsburgh, Pennsylvania, which aired in November 1920.

4. They lived in Elmwood, U.S.A.

5. Marge was Myrt's daughter.

6. He was Dexter Franklin on *Meet Corliss Archer*.

7. He was Spike Jones and his group was named the City Slickers.

8. The mentalist named Dunninger did this.

9. The door of the *Inner Sanctum* closed—but just until the *next* time it was on the air.

10. He was Lamont Cranston. Only Margot Lane knew him.

RAILROADS (AND WAYS) ALL ABOARD!

What red-blooded American hasn't been thrilled by the unique sound of a steam engine's whistle as it echoes across the countryside? Who hasn't been touched by the miniature wonders of a model-train set? Hold onto your ticket and climb on board as we leave for all points of interest!

1. What was the device that was mounted on the front of engines to remove track obstructions?
2. Define the term "doubleheader."
3. What is the specialized type of railway that takes sightseers up to the heights of such places as Mt. Washington in New Hampshire?
4. To a rail company, what is its "high iron"?
5. How many inches of width are in a standard gauge track?
6. Describe a pantograph.
7. Can you name either of the locomotives which met at the Golden Spike ceremony at Promontory Point, Utah?
8. Where would you find a "glad hand" on a train?
9. Which locomotive, with a wild beast painted on her boiler, was the first practical engine to be used on U.S. rails?
10. Here is a test for real track-trivia experts. Match these locomotives with their wheel arrangements.

I.	American (1848)	A.	4-4-2
II.	Mogul (1850)	B.	4-4-4-
III.	Consolidated (1870)	C.	2-8-2
IV.	Decapod (1890)	D.	2-10-0
V.	Atlantic (1896)	E.	2-8-2
		F.	2-8-0
		G.	2-6-2
		H.	4-6-0-
		I.	2-6-0
		J.	4-4-0

RAILROADS (AND WAYS) ALL ABOARD!

answers

1. It was the cowcatcher, invented in 1831. Though a lasso might have been better for the bovines, the metal frame did do its job on an assortment of obstacles.

2. It is a train that is pulled by two locomotives. In this setup, each engine has a crew. This is the opposite of diesels or electrics, which operate with multiple units as one engine with one crew.

3. It is a cog railway. This system has a rack, or toothed rail, between the regular rails. This rack rail engages with the engine's cog wheels to enable a climb to be made.

4. It is the company's main line.

5. Standard gauge has 56½" (4'8½").

6. It is a device that is attached to the tops of electric trains and cars. It looks somewhat like a folding clotheshorse and is used to pick up the current.

7. They were the *Jupiter* (Union Pacific) and *Number 119* (Central Pacific).

8. The glad hand is the metal coupling, or connection, on the end of an air hose. Such hoses have been used in brake systems.

9. It was the *Stourbridge Lion* and had four oak wheels rimmed with iron tires. It was built at Stourbridge, England, in 1829 and brought to the U.S. on a sailing ship to Honesdale, Pennsylvania. After a single historic run, it was not used there again. Yet, word spread and a precedent was made.

10.

I.	American	(J)	4-4-0
II.	Mogul	(I)	2-6-0
III.	Consolidated	(F)	2-8-0
IV.	Decapod	(D)	2-10-0
V.	Atlantic	(A)	4-4-2

RAILROADS (AND WAYS) THE NEXT STATION

It's a whistle-stop—so you'd better hurry inside for your newspaper, snacks, or that postcard you want to mail. Check that second counter rack for these facts.

1. Complete this rail line's name: ______, Topeka & Santa Fe.
2. Which rail company had a super train called the *Twentieth Century Limited*?
3. Can you name two types of the geared steam locomotives used primarily by logging railroads?
4. If you saw a diesel with green lights mounted on its front hood, what would these lights mean?
5. Describe a funicular railway.
6. How many feet of width can be in a narrow gauge track?
7. According to trackside parlance, what is a "varnish"?
8. Can you name both of the main engines that were involved in the "great locomotive chase"?
9. Which locomotive was the first to pull a train in America? *Clue:* It was not the *Tom Thumb.*
10. Once more, here are famous engines for real rail fans to match with their wheel arrangements.

I.	Prairie (1896)	A.	4-8-4
II.	Articulated (1906)	B.	4-6-4
III.	Mountain (1910)	C.	4-6-6-4
IV.	Berkshire (1925)	D.	2-10-4
V.	Challenger (1936)	E.	2-8-4
		F.	0-6-0
		G.	2-6-6-2
		H.	4-8-2
		I.	4-6-2
		J.	2-6-2

RAILROADS (AND WAYS) THE NEXT STATION

answers

1. It is the *Atchison*, Topeka & Santa Fe.

2. The rail company was the New York Central.

3. They are the Shay and the Heisler. The Shay had three cylinders mounted at a vertical angle on the boiler's right side. These cylinders drove a geared crankshaft. The Heisler had two cylinders. The were set up in a V and linked to a driveshaft.

4. Green lights indicate that another section of the train will soon be following.

5. It is a rail system used on varied inclines. It operates by a series of cables that pull cars up or lower them downward. Pittsburgh, Pennsylvania, has one that is in fine working order.

6. Narrow gauge may have two or three feet. Some Maine lines had two-foot gauge rails. Such lines as the Denver & Rio Grande Western had the three-foot gauge.

7. These passenger cars were made of wood and were given several coats of *varnish* for appearance and weather protection.

8. They were the *General* and the *Texas*. In 1862, Union spies seized the *General* at Big Shanty, Georgia. En route northward to Chattanooga, Tennessee, they were chased by confederates on a rail push-car and three different engines at various times. The *Texas* was the key locomotive used in the pursuit. The spies were caught but they spread havoc and panic on their daring raid.

9. It was the *Best Friend of Charleston.* On a trial run in November 1830, she was the first engine to haul a train (four carloads of passengers).

10. I. Prairie (J) 2-6-2
    II. Articulated (G) 2-6-6-2
    III. Mountain (H) 4-8-2
    IV. Berkshire (E) 2-8-4
    V. Challenger (C) 4-6-6-4

RELIGION (AMERICA)

From podium-pounding pitchmen to the devout and pious faithful, America's religions have flourished in an atmosphere of freedom. There have been both difficult struggles and joyful triumphs as varied beliefs found their place in the mainstream.

1. He was the fictitious hymn-and-Hades salesman whose life depicted many real evangelists' causes.

2. Led by men like John Wesley, these people are often associated with a "handshake."

3. Which international Catholic order combines the name of heroic adventures and one famous explorer?

4. Beginning as a major branch of Calvinist Protestants, this religious group is led by elders (whose name in Latin means "priest").

5. A devout Protestant people once made emotional and physical expressions of faith. From their movements, what derisive term for religious zealots has arisen?

6. Which lady evangelist had a certain style and cleverly used the then new medium of radio to broadcast her version of the Bible?

7. Formerly known as the International Bible Students' Association, this Christian organization is opposed to war and government control of religion.

8. Noted for their unique life-style, plain attire, and moral standards, this Mennonite sect is found mainly in the Midwest.

9. Known as the Campbellites, these folks make the Bible their only basis of faith.

10. What Protestant group came to be named for a dance that was only a part of their overall ritual?

RELIGION (AMERICA)

answers

1. He was Elmer Gantry. In the Sinclair Lewis novel of the same name, the lives of traveling revivalists were meaningfully depicted.

2. They are the Methodists. John and Charles Wesley, George Whitefield, and Francis Asbury were Methodism's major founders and ministers.

3. The Knights of Columbus, which were founded in 1882 as a benevolent organization.

4. They are the Presbyterians. A presbytery is a council of church elders. In the Catholic faith, a presbytery is a priest's house.

5. Holy Roller is the prejudiced term and, ironically, it has come to be the name for the sect as well.

6. She was Aimee Semple McPherson. She had a large following until a series of personal problems tainted her credibility.

7. They are Jehovah's Witnesses. They were founded by Charles Russell. Called Russellites for a time, they also were led by Joseph "Judge" Rutherford.

8. This group is the Amish. They were founded in the seventeenth century by Jacob Ammann as a branch of the Mennonites.

9. They are the Disciples of Christ. Founded by Alexander Campbell in 1809, they have Communion every Sunday and baptize by immersion.

10. This group is the Shakers. They are Utopians who practice certain kinds of celibacy, sharing of property, and some communal living. They were most prominent in the eighteenth and nineteenth centuries.

RELIGION (WORLD)

Whether on ancient tablets or upon cave walls, we are constantly reminded that mankind has sought to know and to believe in a power beyond himself. Here are but a few of the people and the faiths expressing this need for fulfillment.

1. He was born Gautama Siddhartha. But we know him better as ______ or the "Enlightened One."

2. What is the Moslem Holy City?

3. In the Jewish faith, why might a Sachem be described as a dealer in nuptial stock?

4. Named after Menno Simons, this Protestant faith began in sixteenth-century Holland and divided into several sects in Europe and America.

5. If Foïsm isn't Taoism in China, what is it?

6. A person belonging to the Uniat or Byzantine Church is a member of what better-known faith?

7. Can you name the oldest major religion that is currently being practiced?

8. Who is Utnapishtim and how did he get a nail ahead of Noah in the "big boat race"?

9. Which country was the first to make Judaism its national religion?

10. Who were Zoroaster and Zarathustra and what did they have to do with Ahriman and Ormazd?

RELIGION (WORLD)

answers

1. Buddha was the "Enlightened One."

2. It is Mecca.

3. Because he once was quite prominent in the arranging of weddings and was a marriage broker.

4. They are the Mennonites. Menno Simons began to organize and lead this group on a province called Friesland in the Netherlands.

5. It is Buddhism. In Chinese, *Fo* is Buddha.

6. It is the Eastern Orthodox Church.

7. Hinduism is the oldest such religion. Its sources of writings and teachings have been traced to as early as 1500 B.C.

8. Utnapishtim was the "Noah" of a very ancient Sumerian epic. This collection of writings was called the *Epic of Gilgamesh*. Some of the similarities with the biblical account include: A supernatural alarm comparable to God's warning of a deluge; the building of a large vessel; and the sending of birds to test the presence of dry land.

9. It was the kingdom of the Khazars in southern Russia. Once a pagan civilization, the Khazars chose Judaism in the eighth century A.D. The reasons for this choice are uncertain. It may have been done so that they could remain in a noncommitted position between other warring faiths.

10. Zarathustra and Zoroaster were the same person who lived between the sixth and seventh centuries B.C. He founded Zoroastrianism, with its principles contained in the Zend-Avesta. In it, Ormazd (Good) perpetually battles Ahriman (Evil) and Ormazd finally is predicted to triumph.

RIDDLES

Did the earlier riddle of the Sphinx in the mythology section whet your appetite for more? Let's hope so—for it's feast or famine as you try to unravel these roundabout rarities.

1. Why can Ireland be called the world's wealthiest country?
2. If a man gave his eldest daughter a dime, his only son a dime, and his youngest daughter a nickel, what time would it be?
3. What was the largest island in the world before Greenland was discovered?
4. How might one fall over 50 feet and not be seriously harmed?
5. What can turn without ever moving even a millimeter?
6. Which thing can be lengthened by being cut at either or both ends?
7. What has less feet in the summer than in the winter?
8. What can lead to a fever, can help cure it, and can pay the bill, too?
9. Which Shakespearean character might be humorously accused of causing the demise of the most geese, ducks, and chickens in literature?
10. What two trades did all U.S. presidents have?

RIDDLES

answers

1. Because its capital is always Dublin.

2. It would be a quarter to three ($.25 among the three).

3. Greenland was then, too. It just had not been found yet.

4. One might try moving from the front to the back of a crowded bus.

5. Milk often turns this trick.

6. A ditch has this curious quality.

7. An ice skating rink.

8. A draft, or breeze, can chill one and lead to illness. A draft of medicine can be a cure. A bank note, or check for payment, can be called a draft.

9. The villain was Hamlet's uncle, since "he did murder most foul."

10. Of course, they were all presidents. Also, they each have been Cabinet makers.

RIDDLES II

Did the previous test leave you tongue-tied? For another chance, here's a riddle replay.

1. Which travels faster, heat or cold?
2. What has four "eyes" and can run 2,000 miles day or night?
3. Who was the Bible's finest financial wizard?
4. Why is a fine riddle like a well-crafted church bell?
5. What was the smallest continent in the world before Australia was discovered?
6. Which word of three syllables can be said to contain 26 letters?
7. When in English history did Monday come ahead of Sunday?
8. How can you get into a totally locked, windowless apartment when you're alone, have no keys, no tools to pick locks, and can't do any damage?
9. How are corn and potatoes quite similar to sinners?
10. Speaking of biblical phrases, what did Samson mean when he riddled, "Out of the eater came forth meat, and out of the strong came forth sweetness"?

RIDDLES II

answers

1. Heat travels faster. You can catch cold.

2. The Mississippi River does this constantly.

3. The money mind was Pharaoh's daughter. In a rush on a bank, she found a prophet.

4. Because it is often tolled.

5. Europe was the smallest before Australia. Europe still would have had this size ranking if Australia had not been found.

6. The word is alphabet.

7. It happened when the first alphabetized list of the week's days was made.

8. You can jog around the apartment until you're "all in."

9. They either have ears that hear not, or eyes that see not. Sinners have been known to have both shortcomings, simultaneously.

10. In Judges 14:14, Samson fooled thirty folks with this baffler. He had recently killed a lion and had eaten some of its meat. In the lion's remains, Samson had found bees and their honey. Thus, from the eater (lion) came meat and out of the strong (lion also) came sweetness (honey).

SECRETS (MYSTERIES AND SUCH)

It has been said that everybody likes a good mystery. It often seems that almost as many folks can't keep a secret. By putting both of them together, one can come up with quite a curious combination—as follows:

1. The mysterious sinking of this ship led to a U.S. war at the turn of a century.

2. Who was the host of the TV game show where everybody had a secret?

3. Which Western outlaw used the alias Mr. Howard? And why was this name ultimately of no help to him?

4. What terrible secret did the unknowning Mary Mallon take with her around a U.S. city?

5. They were the "cities of gold" sought by many early explorers in the Americas. Can you describe their mystery?

6. Can you identify the mysterious American building with the "raining ceiling"?

7. Who was the World War II spy-oriented fellow named Intrepid?

8. Where was the mysterious "lost city" of the Incas and why was it sought by so many people?

9. What was the World War II discovery known as the "Ultra Secret"?

10. We know that aviatrix Amelia Earhart disappeared in the Pacific. However, was she alone or did someone else share in her mysterious demise?

SECRETS (MYSTERIES AND SUCH)

answers

1. It was the battleship *Maine*. On February 15, 1898, it strangely exploded in Havana's harbor and this created a sensation of war fever in the U.S. Though a Spanish mine was blamed, current ideas range from spontaneous combustion to someone on board smoking too near a gunpowder room.

2. He was Garry Moore, host of *I've Got a Secret.*

3. He was Jesse James. His alias may have hidden his identity from the law. However, a member of his gang, Bob Ford, fatally shot him in the back.

4. Mary Mallon earned the tragic nickname "Typhoid Mary" in 1906 in New York City. She was an unwitting carrier of the dread disease.

5. They were the seven Cities of Cibola. Many Spanish and other explorers sought them, for they were thought to have been built of gold.

6. It is a huge Goodyear airship hangar. Located in Akron, Ohio, it has some 50 million cubic feet of air. During quick temperature changes, clouds have been known to form along its ceiling, with rain resulting.

7. Intrepid was the real Sir William Stephenson. He was a Canadian who led British spy operations.

8. It was Machu Picchu in what is present-day Peru. A fabulous treasure of gold, jewels, etc., was rumored to be stored there. Over the centuries, many lost their fortunes trying to find first the city and then the treasure.

9. This was the English cryptanalysts' success in securing the Nazi cipher machine called Enigma. With this knowledge, they broke many wartime codes.

10. Her infrequently mentioned co-flier, Fred Noonan, vanished with her on their ill-fated flight.

VISUAL QUIZ NUMBER SIX

SEMAPHORE

SEMAPHORE

Semaphore is a communicating method that uses either flags or a special mechanism consisting of a tower and poles (arms). The position of these "arms" indicates an alphabet, numbers, etc. Semaphore was one of the earliest means of of sending secret messages.

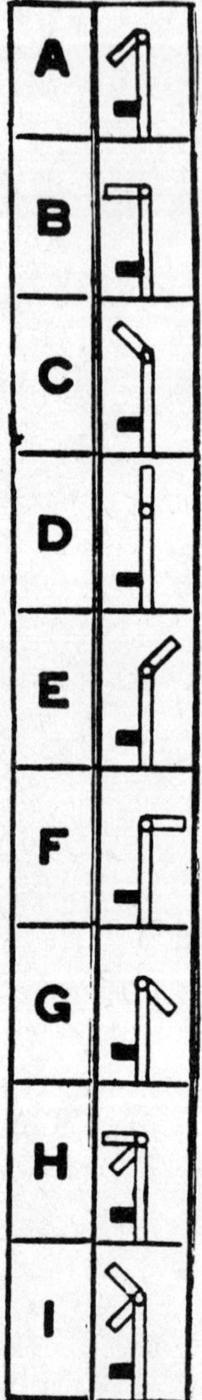

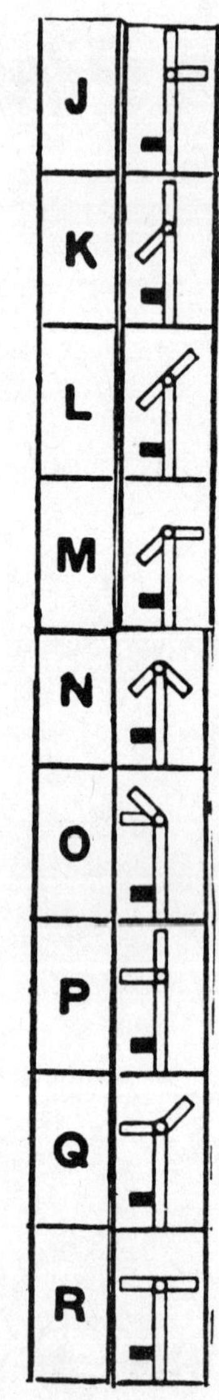

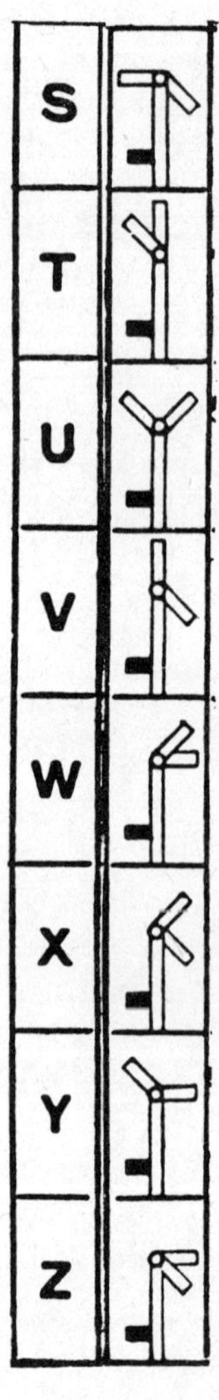

SEMAPHORE

Test your knowledge of espionage by using these semaphore signs to decode these spies' names and facts. Jot down your answers for the code and the name "between the lines" and then turn the page to check them.

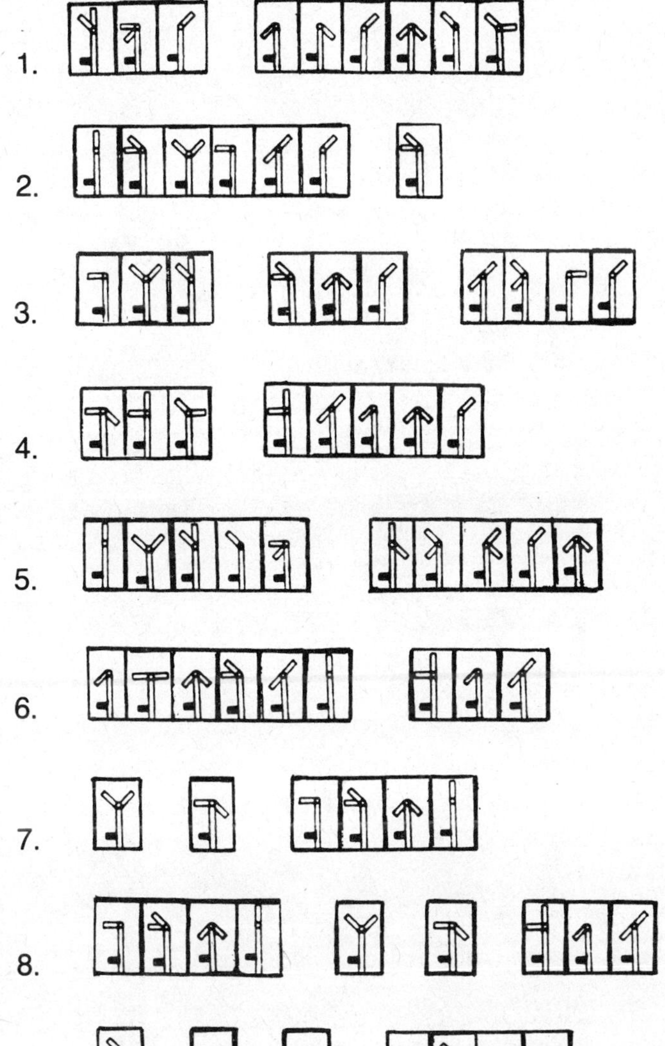

SEMAPHORE

answers

	CODE	NAME
1.	The Agency	CIA
2.	Double 0	James Bond 007
3.	But one life	Nathan Hale
4.	Spy plane	U-2
5.	Dutch Vixen	Mata Hari
6.	Arnold pal	Major John André
7.	U.S. Bond	Matt Helm
8.	Bond U.S. pal	Felix Lighter
9.	OSS boss	"Wild Bill" Donovan
10.	Israel spies	The Mossad

SKY GAZERS

Celestial changes can take eons to happen or they can occur in nanoseconds. Now everything from pulsars to neutrinos have captured the imaginations of star watchers and soothsayers alike. Don your life-support suit and join in this gander at the galaxies.

1. Who was the "Father of the Space Age"?

2. Define the general difference between refracting and reflecting telescopes.

3. Can you name the earth's three major turns?

4. For what purpose was the astrolabe first used?

5. What is a pulsar and how does it differ from other space bodies?

6. Which planet could be called "lazy"?

7. Why isn't Pluto the most distant planet from the sun in our solar system now (1985)?

8. What lady astronomer shelved the books of a Nantucket library and left to make a mark for herself among the stars?

9. Describe a "black hole."

10. Define the following phrase and its meaning to astronomers: Oh, be a fine girl; kiss me right now, sweetheart.

SKY GAZERS

answers

1. He was Dr. Robert Goddard. In 1926, he launched the first rocket with liquid fuel. It climbed to a height of 41 feet. (This seems so short now, but what a feat it was then!)
2. A reflecting telescope has a concave mirror at the lower end of its tube. This mirror receives the light and reflects it toward the focus at the tube's top. A refracting telescope has an object glass that is a double-convex lens. This lens makes light rays converge to a focus, thus forming an image that is magnified by a double-convex eyepiece.
3. The earth turns about its axis (rotation), the sun (revolution), and its center of gravity.
4. The astrolabe (Greek: *astron*, a star, and *lambanein*, to take) once was an instrument used to find a star's altitude. It was replaced by the sextant.
5. A pulsar is a celestial body that emits quick radio-wave pulses. This is in opposition to the more level amounts of radiation given off by other galactic bodies.
6. Uranus can be called "lazy" in that it leans approximately 98° in its solar revolution. In a sense, it lies on its side.
7. Because Neptune now is and has been the most distant since December 1978. At that time, Pluto crossed Neptune's orbit and Neptune's planetary path moved toward its farthest extension. By 1999 they will move back into more familiar configurations.
8. Maria Mitchell became the first female member of the American Academy of Arts and Sciences after discovering a new comet in 1847. She also became Vassar College's first astronomy professor.
9. "Black holes," discovered in 1975, are collapsed stars of extreme density. They are invisible because their gravity is so strong that not even light can escape.
10. Stars are categorized by their spectra. The listing of spectra involves varied wavelengths and colors associated with the stars' different temperatures. To list a decreasing order of temperature, astronomers compile the spectra as O, B, A, F, G, K, M, R, N, S. Astronomers remember these letters by using the following phrase: "*O*h, *B*e *A* *F*ine *G*irl; *K*iss *M*e *R*ight *N*ow, *S*weetheart."

TELL ME ABOUT IT

What more needs to be said? Give it your best shot!

1. This is the sport with the "built-in jewel."
2. In literature, he was known as the "man of bronze" and might be nicknamed the "medical hunk."
3. Whose story is the Tale of the Tape?
4. She was the Hawaiian volcano goddess.
5. Would you use powder or a spray to quash a pesky anapest?
6. He was Tarzan's son in the Edgar Rice Burroughs' books.
7. What can have a point to parry or be a means of finding one's quarry?
8. Can you describe a torii and its significance for a prominent religion?
9. Their distinctive jingle signaled the approach of both villains and heroes in the old West. They were the wheels on the ends of cowboys' spurs.
10. On June 5, 1917, this number became the first official U.S. draft number.

TELL ME ABOUT IT

answers

1. Of course, it's baseball and its diamond.
2. His name was Doc Savage.
3. This is the list of comparative measurements between boxers before a match.
4. She was Pele.
5. Neither. An anapest is a poetic metrical foot of two short syllables followed by a long one.
6. He was Korak (he was called Boy in the movies).
7. It is a foil. It can be a fencing sword or the name for the tracks of an animal.
8. A torii is the gateway to a Shinto temple. It consists of two uprights that support a curved lintel and a straight crosspiece below the lintel.
9. They were rowels. They had sharp, projecting points.
10. It was number 258. At a time of patriotic fervor, many men wished they had it.

THEATER THOUGHTS

Whether in local theater groups, or Off-Off Broadway, the spirit of the theater is alive and flourishing in countless ways. Here is but a sample of interesting facts from this ever-curious subject.

1. This is the nickname for the theater district on Broadway near Times Square.
2. What does the word "dramaturgy" have to do with this section?
3. In theater parlance, what is the parquet?
4. Can you name the prominent theater award that is given for excellence in several categories? Also, for whom is it named?
5. What is the setting for Thornton Wilder's *Our Town?*
6. Please identify Eugene O'Neill's only comedy.
7. What was the unique form of theater begun in Japan in the 1600s?
8. He had the lead role in *The Great White Hope*. But who was he portraying?
9. What was the full name and the profession of Major Barbara?
10. Who was *Waiting for Godot?* At what time did Godot finally arrive?

THEATER THOUGHTS

answers

1. It is "The Great White Way."

2. Dramaturgy is the art of producing or writing plays.

3. The parquet is a theater's main floor.

4. It is the Tony. This award is named for Antoinette Perry, who founded the American Theater Wing.

5. Grovers' Corners, New Hampshire, is the setting.

6. *Ah Wilderness* was O'Neill's lone comedy.

7. It is Kabuki theater, which has particular stylistic rituals for its plots and actors.

8. James Earl Jones was the male lead. He played the part of Jack Johnson, the first black heavyweight champion, in 1908.

9. The Major was Barbara Undershaft, an officer of the Salvation Army.

10. Estragon and Vladimir did the waiting in the Samuel Beckett play. Godot never arrived.

TONIGHT, MR. CARSON

What better way is there to complete a day (or begin it, depending on your profession) than to enjoy the experience of *The Tonight Show*? Yet, though it has been such an influential part of television, what do we really know about its past? Furthermore, what do we know about the man who, to so many, is *The Tonight Show*?

1. Can you name the year when Mr. Carson's permanent association with *The Tonight Show* began?
2. Who was Jack Paar's main announcer?
3. Who were the primary "men on the street" interviewed by Steve Allen?
4. On what programs did Mr. Carson and Mr. Ed McMahon first form a team?
5. Which late-night presentation can be called *The Tonight Show*'s granddaddy?
6. Regarding important calendar events, what do Nairobi African apes and a man named Percy Dovetonsils have to do with October 1, 1956?
7. When was the actual name *Tonight* used as a title and who was the host at that time?
8. Mr. Carson once presided over a match between Misty and Oink. Just who exactly were they?
9. Dagmar was a regular on early 1950s programs. But do you remember what her real name was?
10. Can you describe the first of the "dream sequence" segments in which Mr. Carson participated in the early 1960s?

TONIGHT, MR. CARSON

answers

1. The year was 1962 and the day was October 1.

2. Hugh Downs, now associated with the ABC program *20/20*, was Jack Paar's announcer during Mr. Paar's era from July 29, 1957, to March 30, 1962.

3. The men were "nervous" Don Knotts, Louis Nye as "campy" Gordon Hathaway, and "forgetful" Tom Poston, who couldn't remember his name.

4. They first worked together on the *Who Do You Trust?* game show of the 1950s. Its previous title had been *Do You Trust Your Wife?*

5. It was *Broadway Open House,* which began on NBC on May 29, 1950. Jerry Lester and Morey Amsterdam were two of the more prominent hosts, among others.

6. On October 1, 1956, comedian Ernie Kovacs became a first-time guest host. Soon, he brought his hilarious apes and the Dovetonsils' routines into the show. For some months he continued his special brand of humor on both Monday and Tuesday nights.

7. On September 27, 1954, Steve Allen began hosting with the title, *Tonight!* Soon the Hudson Theater on Broadway became the program's most permanent home in that period of broadcasting.

8. Misty was a 350-pound pony and Oink was a 600-plus-pound porker. They were matched in a "smarts" contest. Misty counted with her hoof and shook hands/hoofs by command. Yet Oink rolled out his personal performer's carpet and sang a medley of songs, including Popeye's theme and "The Blue Danube Waltz." Many in the audience thought the hammy one had won.

9. Dagmar was one of the regulars on *Broadway Open House.* Her real name was Jenny Lewis.

10. Mr. Carson's first "dream sequence" was to pitch against some of the best of the New York Yankees in a segment at Yankee Stadium. This feature was shown on October 5, 1962.

TONIGHT, MR. CARSON II

It's not time to sign off, yet. Much has transpired in the history of late-night television. Here are more interesting items from the files of the kinescope and videotape archives.

1. Jack Paar's wife and daughter were the subjects of many of his monologues. Can you give their names?

2. What do Milton DeLugg, Skitch Henderson, Doc Severinsen, and Jose Melis have in common?

3. During Steve Allen's years, which announcer provided the audible weather forecast facts that were visually pointed out by a shapely nurse?

4. In the Jack Paar era, which "Pixie from Paris" read the baseball scores and called the errors *faux pas*?

5. Which dancing star of the 1940s gained an even brighter aura with a top-tap performance that Mr. Carson hosted in the 1960s? *Clue*: She starred in *Rosalie* and *Sensations of 1945*.

6. Mr. Carson's fitness foresight was evident when he did exercises with a health instructor who had the initials D.D. Can you name her?

7. Which movie-making prestidigitator called Mr. Carson forward to be "cut up" long before he even had begun thinking about his monologues?

8. Speaking of magic, was there ever an actual book of legerdemain that influenced "The Great Carsoni"?

9. Why was the city of Omaha, Nebraska, important to both late-night TV in general and Mr. Carson in particular?

10. How did a door, which wouldn't "break," give Mr. Carson the chance for the big break that brought him out of the "cellar"?

TONIGHT, MR. CARSON II

answers

1. Miriam and daughter, Randy, provided much popular material for Jack's and their mutual fans.

2. From *Broadway Open House* to the current day, these men have served at various times as music directors.

3. Gene Rayburn announced and gave some news and weather. When he was incapacitated by hepatitis, a clever plan enabled him to phone in the weather on live audio while a model in nurse's attire provided the visuals. By the way, there was "always" snow in Ironwood, Michigan.

4. Geneviève was the funny fracturer of English. In 1957 she was to have appeared as a singer. But her way with words was noted and she became a regular.

5. Eleanor Powell tapped her way into a comeback and joined pro dancer John Bubbles in a successful duo that night.

6. Debby Drake is the lovely fitness expert.

7. During World War II, while awaiting induction, Mr. Carson was in San Diego. There he was called forward as a volunteer to participate in a magic act of none other than Orson Welles. Mr. Carson was "sawed" in half then, but has since gotten in his own "cuts" on subsequent shows featuring both men.

8. There's no sleight of hand here. Indeed, he was quite highly inspired by *Hoffman's Book of Magic*. It was a key reference work on the subject that he read in his preteen years.

9. Mr. Carson had his first TV show, *The Squirrel's Nest*, on WOW-TV in Omaha. Also, in the early 1950s, Omaha was the western terminus of the coaxial cable. This cable brought network programs to station affiliates beyond the New York City area.

10. In 1954, comedian Red Skelton was hurt when a breakaway prop door failed to open. Mr. Skelton knew about Mr. Carson's local California show called *Carson's Cellar.* Red asked Mr. Carson to substitute for him. Everything worked right and a new page of TV history was to become volumes.

TUBE TEST

It has been called everything from a "magic box" to a "vast wasteland." Whatever its description, television is a central part of American life. Take this test to see if you are a boob brain or watching whiz. In this case, both nicknames put you at the top of the tube.

1. He entertained the Peanut Gallery with a seltzer bottle and his only spoken words were "Goodbye, kids."

2. He was the former newspaper columnist who became a successful variety-show host.

3. He is the host of PBS's *Masterpiece Theater*.

4. He is the first black person to have a leading role in a prime-time program. Can you name him?

5. On his popular 1960s show, one followed the progress of the bouncing ball. Who is he?

6. Milton Berle was known as "Mr. Television." On which program did he begin to earn this title?

7. Who was the family that *Father Knows Best*?

8. He was the star of the 1950s crime-busters show *Highway Patrol*.

9. *The Man from U.N.C.L.E.* was a spy/adventure series with unusual twists. So, please define its acronym.

10. The first successful TV broadcast occurred where?

TUBE TEST

answers

1. He was Clarabell on the *Howdy Doody Show*.

2. He was Ed Sullivan. His original show's title was *Toast of the Town.*

3. Alistair Cooke is the host.

4. Bill Cosby was a secret agent in *I Spy*.

5. Mitch Miller had the popular musical show.

6. It was on the *Texaco Star Theater.*

7. It was the Anderson family and Robert Young played their popular Dad.

8. Broderick Crawford was the man.

9. It was the *u*nited *n*etwork *c*ommand for *l*aw *e*nforcement.

10. The first successful TV broadcast occurred in London in 1936.

TUBE TEST (ANOTHER CHANNEL)

The selector knob has been turned to give you a new chance to choose from these stars and shows.

1. Which program had a boy with a strange nickname who never seemed to learn from his mistakes?

2. This 1950s variety feature had performers who sang America's top tunes in settings that often matched the songs' themes.

3. Which show was influenced by the Beatnik movement in the late 1950s and early 1960s?

4. It was the Playhouse of TV's early days. Can you give its proper number?

5. They were the first two people to appear on the cover of *TV Guide*.

6. Set in San Francisco, this pioneering drama had leads named Dagmar and Nels.

7. She was *My Little Margie*.

8. This program holds the record for being the longest continuously running show in U.S. history.

9. He played the role of Barnabas Collins on the gothic melodrama *Dark Shadows*.

10. Who has been credited with inventing television?

TUBE TEST (ANOTHER CHANNEL)

answers

1. It was *Leave It to Beaver*. The role of Beaver Cleaver was played by Jerry Mathers.

2. The show was *Your Hit Parade*.

3. *Dobie Gillis* was that program.

4. It was the award-winning series *Playhouse 90*.

5. Lucille Ball appeared with her infant son, Desi Arnaz, Jr. By the way, did you know that Lucille Ball once had the nickname "Technicolor Tessie"? Well, whether or not anyone recalls that sobriquet, everyone will remember *I Love Lucy*.

6. *I Remember Mama* was one of the earliest such dramas on TV. In terms of plots and character development, it compares quite well with today's shows.

7. She is Gale Storm. Her *The Gale Storm Show* aired from 1956 to 1959.

8. Beginning in 1947, it is the interview-oriented program *Meet the Press*.

9. Jonathan Frid played the role of the sinister Collins.

10. In 1926, John Logie Baird, a Scottish inventor, presented what is judged to be the first successful demonstration of television.

U.S. PRESIDENTS

From George Washington until today, they have been a source of both consternation and admiration. Cast your ballot for the correct choice.

1. He lost six major election bids, jobs, and a business before becoming President.
2. He was the youngest man to become Chief Executive.
3. Which White House occupant was the first to be born in a hospital?
4. Which man became Chief Justice of the Supreme Court after his Presidency?
5. He was the first man born in the United States who later became President.
6. In a true "poverty to power" story, this runaway servant and tailor's apprentice achieved the Oval Office.
7. Which Chief Executive should have been praised for his "double-handed" efforts?
8. Who was the single Oval Office occupant to remain a bachelor?
9. How did Miss Frances Folsom affect the status of the only other bachelor in the White House?
10. Our Presidents have been called many names. However, some select nicknames have remained. Can you match the man with his sobriquet?

I.	"His Rotundity"	A.	Andrew Jackson
II.	"Withered Applejohn"	B.	Franklin Delano Roosevelt
III.	"Old Rough and Ready"	C.	John Adams
IV.	"The Little Magician"	D.	Warren Harding
V.	"His Accidency"	E.	E. Zachary Taylor
		F.	James Madison
		G.	Chester Arthur
		H.	Martin Van Buren
		I.	Millard Fillmore
		J.	Rutherford Hayes

U.S. PRESIDENTS

answers

1. He was Abraham Lincoln. He lost in elections on all levels of state and national politics and also went bankrupt. Yet, in spite of it all, he rose to the heights of glory.

2. He was Teddy Roosevelt. When he became President after McKinley's assassination, he was just 43 days short of his 43rd birthday.

3. Jimmy Carter was the first. All those before him were born in private residences or surroundings.

4. He was William Howard Taft and he often remarked that he was most happy in his judicial role.

5. Martin Van Buren, our eighth Chief Executive, was born after the colonial period when the United States had come into existence as a nation.

6. Our seventeenth President, Andrew Johnson, once had been an indentured servant before he escaped. Among a variety of odd jobs, he apprenticed as a tailor and became a skilled one, too.

7. James Garfield was our first left-handed leader. Being ambidextrous and having a knowledge of Latin and Greek, he had the unique ability to write with both hands in both languages simultaneously.

8. James Buchanan has been the only bachelor to remain so during his White House years.

9. She married Grover Cleveland. Frances was his 21-year-old ward and became a popular First Lady.

10.
    I. "His Rotundity" John Adams
    II. "Withered Applejohn" James Madison
    III. "Old Rough and Ready" Zachary Taylor
    IV. "The Little Magician" Martin Van Buren
    V. "His Accidency" Rutherford Hayes

U.S. PRESIDENTS II

Here is a second compilation of just some of the curious facts about our leaders.

1. Large majorities "liked" him in the 1950s.

2. He was the first Chief Executive who was born in the twentieth century.

3. Who was the only man to serve two nonconsecutive terms?

4. She actually was the President in all but title during her husband's lengthy illness.

5. He was the first man born after the Civil War to occupy the Oval Office.

6. He was the first Chief Executive who was born west of the Mississippi River.

7. Which White House occupant served in the U.S. House of Representatives after his Presidency?

8. For a time in 1841, three men were President. Can you name them and describe the situation?

9. Who was David Rice Atchison and how did he manage to be our twelfth Chief Executive for a day?

10. Here are a few more Presidential nicknames for your choice of votes!

I.	"Old Veto"	A.	Calvin Coolidge
II.	"Dark Horse"	B.	U. S. Grant
III.	"Iceberg"	C.	Benjamin Harrison
IV.	"Napoleon"	D.	Lyndon Baines Johnson
V.	"Silent"	E.	William McKinley
		F.	W. H. Harrison
		G.	James K. Polk
		H.	Thomas Jefferson
		I.	James Monroe
		J.	John Tyler

U.S. PRESIDENTS II

answers

1. He was Dwight David "Ike" Eisenhower. Not only did his nickname rhyme well but his life-style and leadership fit the 1950s mood.

2. He was John F. Kennedy. At the age of 43, he was our youngest *elected* to the White House.

3. Grover Cleveland served during these years: 1885 to 1889 and 1893 to 1897. He led America during a time of rapid economic and social change.

4. She was Edith Galt Wilson. When her husband, Woodrow, was stricken with a debilitating stroke, she quite capably did his work and greatly aided the nation.

5. Born on November 2, 1865, he was Warren G. Harding. Swayed by political cronies, his administration was tainted by widespread corruption.

6. He was our thirty-first President, Herbert Hoover.

7. John Quincy Adams served in the Oval Office from 1825 to 1829. In 1830, he was elected to the House by his Massachusetts constituency.

8. In 1841, March 3rd marked the end of Martin Van Buren's term. William Henry Harrison was inaugurated the next day. However, he died after only 32 days and was succeeded by John Tyler. In five weeks, three men had led the U.S.

9. The year was 1849 and James Polk's term had been completed on a Sunday at noon. Newly elected Zachary Taylor did not take his official oath until Monday. Vice President George Dallas was no longer president of the Senate. Missouri's Senator Atchison was elected by the Senate to have Dallas's position. Therefore, Atchison became President according to constitutional provisions for the interim time.

10.
    I. "Old Veto" John Tyler
    II. "Dark Horse" James K. Polk
    III. "Iceberg" Benjamin Harrison
    IV. "Napoleon" William McKinley
    V. "Silent" Calvin Coolidge

UBIQUITOUS U'S

The letter U doesn't seem all that common except when one considers all its possibilities. Here are some of the more interesting and *unusu*al.

1. To the philosoper Nietzsche, he was Ubermensch. *Clue:* To Americans, he's faster than a speeding bullet.
2. How many udders does a normal cow have?
3. What four-stringed instrument is translated as "flea" in the language of its native origin?
4. It is both an overcoat and an Irish province.
5. What nickname was derived from the stamp of a meat inspector during the War of 1812?
6. Which slang word means a great number, very many, etc.?
7. In Latin this word means little grandfather. It also is slang for a pawnbroker.
8. Scientists consider it a perfect shadow whereby no direct light comes from the illuminating source.
9. To ancient peoples it was the farthest northern region, beyond the limits of their explorations.
10. In folklore, this female water spirit was able to secure a soul by marrying a mortal and bearing his child.

UBIQUITOUS U'S

answers

1. To Nietzsche, Ubermensch was Superman. This being was supposed to be an idealized, superior human regarded as the ultimate goal of evolutionary survival.

2. A cow has one udder. Each udder can have more than one teat.

3. It is the ukulele, which means flea in Hawaiian.

4. Ulster is the answer. It is a long, heavy, belted overcoat often made of Irish frieze. The province is divided between Ireland and Northern Ireland.

5. The nickname is Uncle Sam. It was derived from the stamp of one Samuel Wilson. He was a meat inspector who checked barrels with the initials: U.S.-E.A. this represented the *U*nited *S*tates and *E. A*nderson, who was a food contractor. Soldiers turned the U into uncle and, since they knew Sam Wilson personally, they nicknamed him their Uncle Sam.

6. Umpteen is the word. It is also known as umpsteen.

7. The word is uncle.

8. An umbra is a complete shadow to physicists. It also can be the dark cone of a shadow that projects from a planet which is on the opposite side of the sun.

9. Ultima Thule was the ancients' name for distant, unknown regions.

10. An undine (Latin: *unda*, a wave) was the mortal-seeking sprite.

VARIETY PACK

Here are a variety of unusual ingredients to put in either your hodgepodge or potpourri stews. You have a choice of True-False, Multiple Guess, or Fill-in-the-Blanks.

1. What are you judging when you consider: balance, color, body, and aroma? *Clue:* You are not judging a lithe, tanned, or sweaty gymnast, at least not here.
2. A dickey can be a donkey, a child's bib, a small bird, and a carriage driver's seat. True or False?
3. We know that Samuel Clemens's pen name was ______. However, what did this term mean on the Mississippi?
4. Named for a New York Catskill's resort, Vaudeville was popular in the U.S. in the 1800s and the early 1900s. True or False?
5. In Savannah, Georgia, in 1912, what did Juliette Low do to contribute to the phrase, "That's the way the cookie crumbles"?
6. This British Tommy is like America's man with his name on many sample forms. Uncle Sam's man is John ______. Can you give Tommy's full name, too?
7. If you had a beaver, a gorget, a pauldron, and a tasse, what could you possibly do with them?
   (A) Make a hat (B) Sew a dress (C) Begin an armor suit
8. Though this bird doesn't have feet, it can stand high on many a crest.
9. What was the basic meaning of the word "derry" in old ballads?
   (A) Town (B) Nothing at all (C) Good
10. Many people have blind spots when it comes to habits and vices. But where do we all have one?

VARIETY PACK

answers

1. These are factors in wine tasting.

2. True. A dickey can be all of these things—and a detachable shirt front, too.

3. *Mark Twain.* It meant "safe water" at a depth of two fathoms.

4. False. Vaudeville was named for a valley in France. It was the *Vau-de-Vire*, the valley of the Vire River in Normandy. This region was noted for the popular songs of the people.

5. She founded the Girl Scouts. In England, they had been called the Girl Guides. All jokes about cookies aside, it is a most worthy organization.

6. *Doe*. Tommy Atkins is England's bloke for all reasons.

7. (C). Begin an armor suit. These are just some of the separate items necessary for the complicated medieval apparel.

8. It is a martlet. This was a bird used in heraldry on family crests/coats of arms.

9. (B). Nothing at all. It was used for rhyming convenience in many rounds and ditties.

10. In our heads, at the point where the optic nerve enters the retina.

VICE PRESIDENTS

Often the object of cruel humor, these men also have been a heartbeat from the Presidency. How much do you recall about them?

1. He was our first Vice President.

2. Who was Thomas Jefferson's Vice President and had a promising career until political intrigues and dueling ruined him?

3. His grandfather was Grover Cleveland's V.P., but he twice ran unsuccessfully for President. *Clue:* John Q. Public liked Ike more.

4. Can you name the three men who were FDR's V.P.s?

5. Who was the first V.P. to succeed to the Presidency after a Chief Executive's death?

6. Regarding #5, can you name the eight other men who succeeded to the Oval Office in tragic situations?

7. Who were the three V.P.s who became Presidents and later died on July 4th, within a few years of one another?

8. He was Woodrow Wilson's Vice President. However, he is best remembered for linking the nation's well-being with a smoking product. Can you name him and his famous quote?

9. He was James Madison's V.P. However, his name has been more often connected with a political redistricting maneuver. Please identify him and this controversial plan.

10. Who was the last Whig Vice President?

VICE PRESIDENTS

answers

1. He was John Adams, who became a very influential Chief Executive in his own right.

2. Aaron Burr ambitiously sought the Presidency. However, after the disputed Presidential election of 1800, a setback in the New York governor's race, and the fatal shooting of Alexander Hamilton, Burr embarked on a reckless scheme. He allied himself with men who sought to make a new nation of western territories. Though acquitted of treason, Burr's career was ruined.

3. He was Adlai E. Stevenson (1900–1965). His grandfather was also Adlai E. Stevenson (1835-1914). The latter was Grover Cleveland's Vice President from 1893 to 1897.

4. They were John Nance Garner (1933–1941), Henry A. Wallace (1941–1945), and Harry Truman (1945).

5. He was John Tyler, who was also the first Vice President of the Whig Party.

6. The eight others were: Millard Fillmore, Andrew Johnson, Chester Arthur, Theodore Roosevelt, Calvin Coolidge, Harry Truman, Lyndon Johnson, Gerald Ford.

7. They were Thomas Jefferson (July 4, 1826), John Adams (July 4, 1826), and James Monroe (July 4, 1831).

8. He was Thomas R. Marshall, who said, "What this country needs is a good five-cent cigar."

9. Elbridge Gerry has this odd distinction. He was V.P. from 1813 to 1817. However, when he was the governor of Massachusetts, his name was used to create the term "gerrymander." This referred to political favoritism with changing of boundaries of election districts to benefit one party over another.

10. He was Millard Fillmore, who served with Zachary Taylor. V.P. Fillmore later became our thirteenth President.

WESTERNS (GOOD, BAD, AND HOMELY)

The hero and the villain face each other on the muddy street. The numerous but cowardly townsfolk have fled to safety, and to watch. One woman doesn't look. She is Joisey Lil and she waits in the Long Sip Saloon. But, the question is—for whom does she wait?

1. What were the Lone Ranger's "calling cards"?
2. This former Pennsylvanian made more than a hundred westerns in his heydey. *Clue:* His name sounds like something stirred.
3. They were Butch Cassidy's gang.
4. What do Henry McCarty and William Bonny have in common?
5. Can you give the real name of the man who portrayed Hopalong Cassidy?
6. This Arizona native was known for a time as the "last singing cowboy."
7. Can you name the famous 1881 "shootout" corral and those who opposed one another?
8. Did Lash LaRue wear a black or a white hat?
9. Why is the name of stagecoach driver Charlie Parkhurst of historic significance?
10. Who was the real "hanging judge" of Arkansas?

WESTERNS (GOOD, BAD, AND HOMELY)
answers

1. *T*hey were Silver Bullets.

2. *He* was Tom Mix. True to casting, he was a real-life U.S. marshall.

3. *E*veryone's favorite thieves, the Hole-in-the-Wall Gang.

4. *H*enry and William were Billy the Kid's other names.

5. *E*asy-going hero William Boyd is the man.

6. *R*ex Allen was given this title for such songs as "Streets of Laredo" and "Crying in the Chapel."

7. *O*.K. was the corral's name. The opponents were: Wyatt, Virgil, and Morgan Earp, and Doc Holliday versus the McLaury and Clanton brothers and Billy Claiborne.

8. He wore a black hat since he dressed in black. And in early 1900s movies, he used his bullwhip on the West's most dastardly villains.

9. Charlie Parkhurst drove a stage through California's wildest Gold Rush days and once killed two highwaymen. When Charlie passed away on his Santa Cruz cattle ranch, he was discovered to be a woman. *She* really came a *long* way, baby!

10. He was Judge Isaac Parker. At Fort Smith, Arkansas, his authority extended over a wide area including Indian territories. He had a huge gallows built upon which twelve desperados could be hanged at one time.

P.S. Have you been wondering about the italicized letters? Group the first three in order, then group the next four in order. You'll quickly see who has won Lil's heart.

WHAT ME CARE?

Yes, it's very tempting to give up on your search for knowledge. But be brave—be true to the challenge. Just think about all the clever comments you can make at highbrow parties. Why, your agile, well-conditioned brain will put the others' ungainly gray matter to shame! So, go forward, move onward in your quest!

1. In Transcendental Meditation, what is the name of your personal incantation?

2. Once used as a fire retardant, this substance is the single form of rock that can be woven.

3. In 1945, yet another fashion was initiated with a debatable "12 inches from the floor." Can you name this style?

4. A device called a clepsydra once competed with sand and sun to record a very precious commodity. Can you describe the what and why of it?

5. Why would a man need to be concerned about hyphens if he wanted to build a "love nest" with a "Lucy Stoner"?

6. Their nickname made them sound like a dainty social club. However, they were as tough as the coal they mined day and night.

7. In philately, why is having one or more items with O.G. considered a G.O.O.D. thing?

8. This "horizon hound" has spooked even the hardiest hunter in the woodlands.

9. One might think of this phrase as a dance step. However, it concerns imbibing and is known as "heel tap." Can you define it?

10. If you build an acrolith of a famous woman who didn't have "clay feet," why would you still have to worry about termites?

WHAT ME CARE?

answers

1. It is your mantra.

2. It is asbestos. A silicate of calcium and magnesium, asbestos occurs in lengthy, threadlike fibers.

3. This was the "new look" of the Paris designer Christian Dior. But—oh how the gam gazers howled at its arrival in the States!

4. A clepsydra was a water clock. This device measured the "precious commodity" (time) by the marked flow of the water through a small opening.

5. A "Lucy Stoner" is an advocate of married women keeping their own names. Therefore, any man courting someone of this persuasion should be considering hyphenated last names quite seriously. Lucy Stone was Mrs. Henry Brown Blackwell, an American suffragist.

6. They were Molly Maguires. Especially from 1865 to 1875, these Irish-American miners in eastern Pennsylvania promoted industrial reforms. Their predecessors (of the same name) were land-reform protesters in Ireland in the 1840s. They sometimes disguised themselves as women.

7. O.G., or *o*ld *g*um, is a "good" thing to find when one is a philatelist (stamp collector).

8. This odd optical image is actually a bright spot at the horizon during a fog.

9. It is the trace of liquor that may remain in a glass after drinking.

10. An acrolith is a statue with a head, hands, and feet of stone. However, its trunk is wooden. Thus the need for termite precautions.

WHAT'S OUR LINE?

Here is the final segment of our homage to great TV quiz programs of the past. Though this concept is familiar, it can be puzzling. So, as usual, be careful.

1. I once performed in a Wild West show in Africa. I did rope tricks and told jokes. I was called the "Cherokee Kid."
2. He was one of early America's great orators. He made the "most of treason" and chose liberty in spite of great danger.
3. We began as a team in 1936. We performed on the Kate Smith Show. Our first movie in 1941 was *Buck Privates.*
4. This person was forgetful in little ways throughout life. After failing a special exam, this individual might have lived a life among paperwork. However, thoughts about the tiny and immense changed everything for this person and others as well.
5. He was born in a cloakroom. He was a bricklayer and avoided a vexing situation. He took over an important seat that had belonged to his father.
6. Research interested this person at an early age. Through many struggles against scientific prejudice, this person prevailed. With a close partner, this individual made important discoveries.
7. Ursula, my first love, rejected me. Cien helped me create *Sorrow,* but we parted, too. Through my many problems, I still saw the starry nights.
8. He found an inspiration for an alternative to change on a South African train. His methods puzzled an empire but led to freedom for millions.
9. This person escaped political persecution and found peace long enough to compose classic works of music that were often sung in someone else's language.
10. She grew up in a volatile time in America. Though prejudice hindered her, too, she served her country. By helping other medical people during a terrible struggle, she achieved a most high and special honor.

WHAT'S OUR LINE?

answers

1. I was Will Rogers, wit, sage, and humorist.
2. He was Patrick Henry, patriot and founding father.
3. We were Abbott and Costello, popular comedians.
4. This person was Albert Einstein, physicist and scholar.
5. He was Winston Churchill, statesman and world leader.
6. This person was Marie Curie. Her partner was her husband, Pierre. Both were scientists.
7. I was Vincent Van Gogh, Impressionist artist.
8. He was Mohandas K. Gandhi, Indian statesman and world leader.
9. This person was Richard Wagner, German composer.
10. She was Dr. Mary Walker. She was the only woman to be awarded the Congressional Medal of Honor for her efforts as a Civil War medic.

VISUAL QUIZ NUMBER SEVEN

WIG-WAG

TURN PAGE

WIG-WAG

Wig-Wag is a method of communicating by means of flags or lights. This system is used by scouts, military personnel, and pathfinders.

WIG-WAG

These phrases and words are associated with noted explorers. Please apply the usual decoding system. Jot down your answers for the code and the explorer "between the lines" and then turn the page to check them.

1.
2.
3.
4.
5.
6.
7.
8.
9.
10.

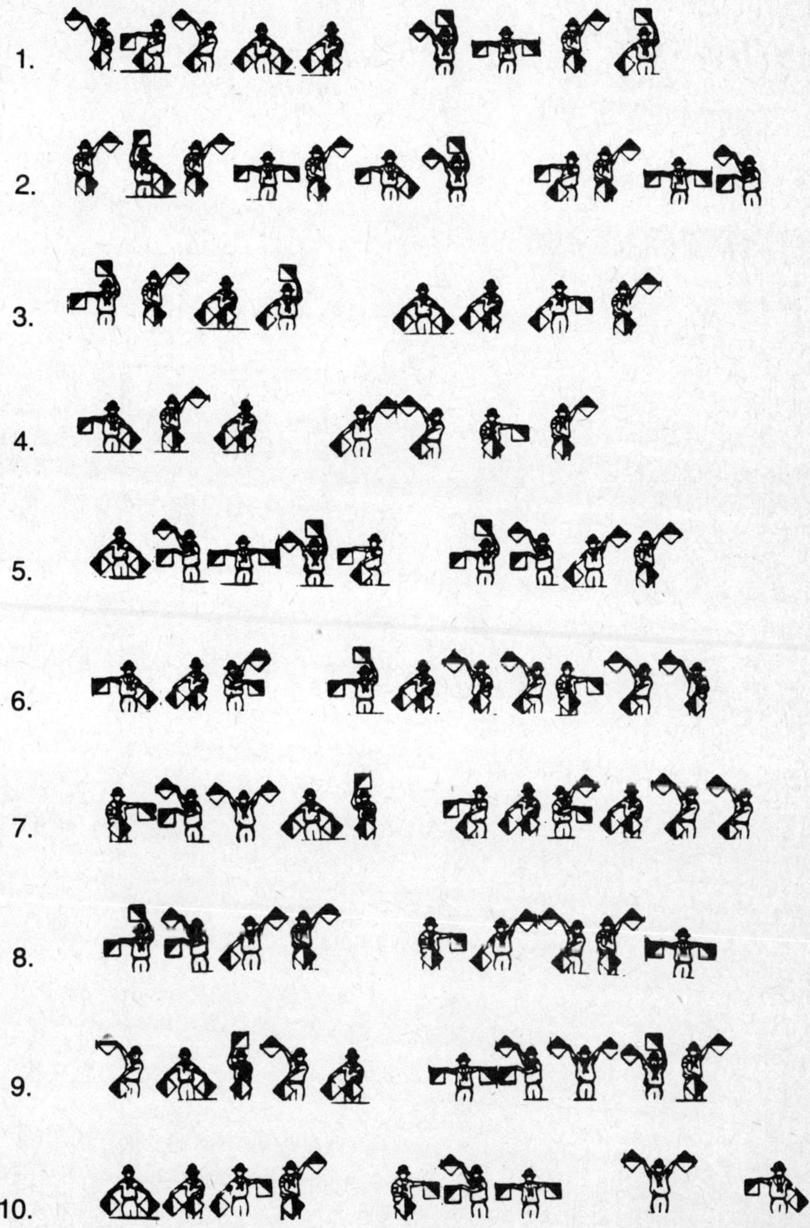

WIG-WAG
answers

	CODE	EXPLORER
1.	China Trek	Marco Polo
2.	Everest Hero	Edmund Hillary
3.	Peak Name	Zebulon Pike
4.	Sea Life	Jacques Cousteau
5.	North Pole	Robert Peary
6.	Saw Pacific	Vasco Balboa
7.	Found Hawaii	Capt. James Cook
8.	Pole Flier	Adm. Richard E. Byrd
9.	India Route	Vasco da Gama
10.	Name for U.S.	Amerigo Vespucci

WILLIAM THE BARD

He has been called everything from the greatest playwright to a clever borrower of others' writings. Whatever, he has lasted through history as the Bard of Stratford-on-Avon.

1. This play about regicide was Shakespeare's shortest.

2. We know the story of the star-crossed lovers, Juliet and Romeo. However, what were their last names?

3. Of which tragedy was Anne Hathaway the heroine?

4. Was Shylock considered a bad merchant for charging a pound of flesh in Venice?

5. What do a moth, a cobweb, and a mustard seed have in common with Shakespeare?

6. In which play was the Bard out of step with time?

7. By what strange name was Robin Goodfellow also known?

8. He was a portly, witty, but sometimes hesitant knight who appeared in both a two-part drama and a comedy.

9. Can you name two of the writers from whom Shakespeare is sometimes accused of borrowing?

10. Regarding #1 above, how did Birnam Wood (part of a forest) get to Dunsinane Castle?

WILLIAM THE BARD

answers

1. It was *Macbeth.* His ambitious wife persuaded him to kill King Duncan.

2. She was Juliet Capulet and he, Romeo Montague.

3. She wasn't a fictitious character of any tragedy. Rather, she was William's wife.

4. Shylock wasn't a merchant, but a moneylender. Antonio was the *Merchant of Venice.*

5. As proper names, Moth, Cobweb, and Mustardseed, they were fairies from *A Midsummer Night's Dream.*

6. In *Julius Caesar,* a striking clock was used in a scene set in a year well before these timepieces existed.

7. Puck was another of his names. In *A Midsummer Night's Dream* as well as English folklore, he was a prankish elf who played tricks on people.

8. He was Sir John Falstaff. He appeared in both *Henry IV* (Parts I and II) and *The Merry Wives of Windsor.*

9. They are Geoffrey Chaucer, who wrote the *Canterbury Tales, and Giovanni Boccaccio, who wrote the Decameron.*

10. The men of McDuff carried the woods' tree branches for protection as they attacked Dunsinane. This was a fulfillment of an earlier prophesy and meant the downfall of the play's central character.

WIT'S END

No, we haven't completed our trivia trek yet. However, if this conglomerated cornucopia doesn't drive you to your wit's end, you're a better person than many, McGee.

1. Freeman Gosden and Charles Correll caused theaters to begin their features a half hour or more later due to their own popularity. How did they acquire such power?

2. They can be types called: set, lag, and machine.

3. How many dancers are involved in the type of ballet known as the *pas seul*?

4. Who would be most likely to make use of a billiken?

5. If there actually is a place called Land's End, where might it be?

6. What isn't so "great" about the Great Karoo?

7. By golly, what did a loblolly boy do?

8. We've defined a pyrrhic victory. With that costly victory in mind, what is a Cadmean victory?

9. What possible value could the word "Volapük" have?

10. Can you define the "Curse of Meleager"? *Clue:* An object removed at his birth was replaced in his later life and spelled his doom.

WIT'S END

answers

1. They were Amos and Andy. Their radio show was so popular that people wanted to hear its completion before they would attend a movie that same evening.

2. They are screws.

3. Only one person dances. In French, *pas seul* means solo dance.

4. A billiken might be used by a child or anyone who likes toys. Billikens were round-based, doll-like figures of a generation ago.

5. There is such a place. Land's End is the name of a cape at England's southwesternmost point.

6. The Great Karoo is a vast, arid wasteland in South Africa. Some controversial efforts have been tried in an attempt to reclaim the land.

7. He was the attendant of a ship's doctor, as in the British navy. Loblolly seems to have an origin in a term for "stiff medicine."

8. It's another wasteful win. It is based on the Greek legend of Cadmus. He was a Phoenician prince who was credited with founding Thebes (after he slew a dragon that was sacred to Mars). He sowed the dragon's teeth and they became warriors. After fighting among themselves, only five were left. They allied themselves with Cadmus to build Thebes.

9. It would be valuable to anyone wishing to learn an artificial language. Volapük was created by one J. M. Schleyer from Baden, Germany, in 1879 as an auxiliary international language.

10. Meleager was one of the Argonauts. At his birth, his mother, Althea, removed a certain log from the royal Calydon fireplace. As long as it wasn't consumed by flames, Meleager would live. However, Meleager killed his quarrelsome maternal uncles and Althea vengefully threw the log onto a fire. Meleager perished, at least indirectly, by his own hand.

X MARKS THIS SPOT

One often thinks of X when crossing something off a list. Yet, there are a number of X facts that often aren't noticed. You guessed it. Here they are.

1. O is the symbol for a hug on a letter. For what does an X stand?
2. What can X in mathematics signify?
3. Which plane was used to break the sound barrier?
4. He was the son of Darius and was a Persian king.
5. She was regarded by some as the prototype of the shrewish wife. Some also believe that she caused her famous husband to drink more than wine.
6. What is a xiphoid process? *Clue:* It is not a photocopying process.
7. What was the first X-rated movie to win an Oscar?
8. In the movie *X, Y, and ZEE,* who were these three?
9. Which awards did the XYZ Affair win?
10. Can you define what XP means to religious scholars?

X MARKS THIS SPOT

answers

1. An X stands for a kiss.

2. It can signify an unknown quantity.

3. The X-1 broke the sound barrier in 1947.

4. He was Xerxes. He defeated the Spartans at the Thermopylae pass, but only with the help of a traitor.

5. She is Xanthippe. In the fifth century B.C., her husband, Socrates, drank hemlock due to political and philosophical reasons. However, some say she did nothing to dissuade him.

6. Xiphoid is derived from the Greek word *xiphoeides,* which means sword-shaped. The xiphoid process is the cartilaginous extension at the lower end of the sternum (breastbone).

7. It was *Midnight Cowboy* (1969).

8. They were Susannah York, Michael Caine, and Liz Taylor.

9. This affair won no awards. It was a naval and diplomatic dispute between the U.S. and France in 1798. X, Y, and Z were unnamed aides of the French minister of foreign affairs, Charles Maurice Tallyrand. The U.S. representatives were told that they would have to pay bribes to Tallyrand (through X, Y, and Z) to secure a settlement. After a harsh U.S. reaction, other means settled the matter.

10. XP represents Christianity or Jesus Christ. These letters are *chi* and *rho,* the first two letters of the name Christos (Greek for Christ).

YIDDISH

Yiddish is defined as a language that is spoken by numerous European Jews and their descendents in various nations. Of course, most dictionaries should add that such interesting and often humorous words have become a part of many countries and their native tongues.

Yiddish is written in Hebrew alphabet characters and is a High German dialect. It contains elements of Polish as well. As you begin, mazel tov!

1. Bagel: (A) Pancake (B) Biscuit (C) Ring-shaped roll
2. Kosher: (A) True (B) Clean (C) Strong
3. Knish: (A) Thief (B) Dumpling (C) Bread
4. Shiksa: (A) Fool (B) Non-Jewish girl (C) Gall
5. Megilla: (A) Long story (B) Argument (C) Mess
6. Mazuma: (A) Cash (B) Argument (C) Luck
7. Nudnik: (A) Pancake (B) Pest (C) Fool
8. Yenta: (A) Honored one (B) Cake (C) Gossip
9. Ish kabibble: (A) Fate (B) I should worry (C) Luck
10. Fresser: (A) Miser (B) Thief (C) Big eater

YIDDISH
answers

1. (C) Ring-shaped roll
2. (B) Clean
3. (B) Dumpling
4. (B) Non-Jewish girl
5. (A) Long story
6. (A) Cash
7. (B) Pest
8. (C) Gossip
9. (B) I should worry
10. (C) Big eater

YOUGHIOGHENY AND THEN SOME

Did you recognize the Youghiogheny as the river that flows from Maryland's mountains and meets the Monongahela River near Pittsburgh, Pennsylvania? If you did, you're well on your way to answering these queries.

1. Can you give the name of the vegetable that is similar to a sweet potato?

2. FDR, Churchill, and Stalin had a highly controversial meeting at this site in February 1945.

3. What is a hunting call that urges the hounds to chase the fox?

4. Which river on the Manchuria-Korea border was a key point of debate in the Korean War?

5. They were a brutish, degraded, manlike people in *Gulliver's Travels*.

6. This specific mocking nickname for a Hollander in the American Colonies became a general nickname for Americans as a people. What was each sobriquet?

7. What is the name for a bridge or whist hand that has no card higher than a nine?

8. This particular comic strip's printing style led to the name for a kind of journalism.

9. This is a slang term for a safecracker.

10. What was the huge ash tree of Norse mythology with limbs and roots that held the universe together?

YOUGHIOGHENY AND THEN SOME

answers

1. It is a yam. Its name derives from the Senegalese word *nyami* (to eat). Yams are edible, starchy roots of climbing tropical plants.

2. The site was Yalta, a port city in the Crimea. Several decisions made here about the post–World War II world led to much debate.

3. Yoicks is the word. No doubt several hunter/riders have gasped "Yikes!" on many a bumpy back road, too.

4. It is the the Yalu River. It was a controversial point beyond which U.S. bombers could not fly while trying to support South Korean forces battling on land.

5. They were the Yahoos.

6. Jan Kaas, or John "Cheese," was a disparaging name for Dutch people in the Colonies. It spread to Englishmen in Connecticut, then to all New Englanders. Eventually the words blended to become *Yankee* to Northerners and then to Americans in general.

7. This card hand is a Yarborough. It was named after the Earl of Yarborough. He had wagered the odds of 1000 to 1 against its occurrence.

8. The comic strip was the "Yellow Kid." It was printed with yellow ink by the *New York World* in 1895. Soon this yellow tint came to be applied to cheap, thrill-creating "journalism" in several newspapers that competed for readers.

9. A yegg is a nimble-fingered thief.

10. This mythological tree was yggdrasill. The name was derived from the Old Norse word *Yggdra Syll* (one of Odin's names).

ZOOLOGY

Earlier, we had some interesting encounters with both familiar animal friends and new acquaintances. Because of the size of the animal kingdom, a reprise has been included here.

1. These animals' most common trait is their "pouch."
2. Which lion gender actually does the most hunting?
3. It is the world's largest living primate.
4. This creature is the largest land carnivore.
5. What is the primary difference between New World monkeys and Old World monkeys?
6. Can you name the bat's three closest aerial rivals?
7. It is the only lizard that makes noises.
8. What unusual trait do cats, giraffes, and camels share?
9. What do the firefly, crayfish, and horned toad have in common?
10. Can you match the column of animals with their respective sounds?

I.	Camel	A.	Gibber	K.	Growl
II.	Beetle	B.	Roar	L.	Screech
III.	Bull	C.	Bellow	M.	Bray
IV.	Seagull	D.	Howl	N.	Tap
V.	Cattle	E.	Trumpet	O.	Drone
VI.	Donkey	F.	Cackle	P.	Drum
VII.	Monkey	G.	Squeal	Q.	Grunt
VIII.	Wolf	H.	Hiss	R.	Low
IX.	Owl	I.	Scream	S.	Clatter
X.	Goat	J.	Chirp	T.	Bleat

ZOOLOGY

answers

1. They are the marsupials.

2. The female of the species contributes approximately 90 percent of the search for game.

3. The gorilla has this distinction.

4. It is the Kodiak bear. Some of them can weigh as much as 1,500 pounds.

5. Old World monkeys (from Asia and Africa) can't hang by their tails. New World monkeys (South and Central America) can suspend themselves by their tails.

6. They are the "flying" phalanger, the "glider" opossum, and the "flying" squirrel. The phalanger is an Australian marsupial that actually leaps to imitate flight. The opossum and the squirrel glide by means of winglike folds of skin, but they do so only for short distances.

7. It is the gecko (Malay: *gekoq*, its echoic cry).

8. These animals share the trait of moving their hind and front legs on one side; then they move the hind and front appendages on the opposite side. Other animals move their appendages diagonally opposed.

9. These creatures are not what their names imply. The fireflies are beetles' relatives. The crustaceans claim the crayfish. A horned toad is a lizard.

10.

I.	Camel	(Q)	Grunt
II.	Beetle	(O)	Drone
III.	Bull	(C)	Bellow
IV.	Seagull	(I)	Scream
V.	Cattle	(R)	Low
VI.	Donkey	(M)	Bray
VII.	Monkey	(A)	Gibber
VIII.	Wolf	(D)	Howl
IX.	Owl	(L)	Screech
X.	Goat	(T)	Bleat

ZOOLOGY II

Our reprise of the animal kingdom continues with more curious creatures for your perusal.

1. This fowl is the most numerous of the domesticated varieties.
2. It is the most venomous spider.
3. It is the mammal found at the highest altitude. *Clue*: Its name also means to talk incessantly.
4. Can you identify the largest fish?
5. This sea mollusk's shell is used for jewelry.
6. What is the special house pet that is a watch dog and guards against the hated cobra?
7. Which animal is the fastest on land over a long distance?
8. What is the tallest dog breed?
9. Which wild bird is the most abundant in the Americas?
10. Match the following gender and animal young with their correct names.

I.	Female Fox	A.	Foal	K.	Pen
II.	Male Cat	B.	Gosling	L.	Clupper
III.	Female Whale	C.	Boar	M.	Ram
IV.	Young Whale	D.	Cob	N.	Gandling
V.	Female Swan	E.	Vixen	O.	Tom
VI.	Male Swan	F.	Cublet	P.	Cygnet
VII.	Young Swan	G.	Fawn	Q.	Bull
VIII.	Young Goose	H.	Cow	R.	Hinny
IX.	Male Sheep	I.	Jenny	S.	Jack
X.	Male Elephant	J.	Calf	T.	Doenall

ZOOLOGY II

answers

1. It is the ever popular chicken.

2. The black widow holds this unenviable distinction.

3. It is the yak, the long-haired wild ox. It can be found at very high altitudes in Tibet and Asia.

4. The whale shark is the answer, and a dangerous predator it is.

5. The abalone's rather spiral shell is lined with mother-of-pearl. This increases its use as a source for jewelry.

6. It is the mongoose (pl. mongooses). It derives from the Marathi word, *mangus,* and is a ferretlike, flesh-eating animal originally from India.

7. The antelope is the fastest at distances of 1,000 yards of more. For shorter distances, the cheetah is the speedster.

8. It is the Irish wolfhound, a large dog with a heavy coat, still used to hunt wolves.

9. It is the often pesky starling, which is noted for its iridescent plumage and was originally native to Europe.

10.

I.	Female Fox	(E)	Vixen
II.	Male Cat	(O)	Tom
III.	Female Whale	(H)	Cow
IV.	Young Whale	(J)	Calf
V.	Female Swan	(K)	Pen
VI.	Male Swan	(D)	Cob
VII.	Young Swan	(P)	Cygnet
VIII.	Young Goose	(B)	Gosling
IX.	Male Sheep	(M)	Ram
X.	Male Elephant	(Q)	Bull

ZOUNDS AND ZYMURGY

With an exclamation of surprise and the name for the chemistry of fermentation, here's hoping you'll zip through this zany segment with a score of a zillion to zilch!

1. It is the slang name for a "zonked-out" person, a drink of mixed rums, and an African Voodoo term.

2. What was the unusually styled men's apparel that became popular among "hep cats" in the 1940s?

3. Please describe the words derived from the acronym ZIP.

4. It is the musical instrument that made the movie, *The Third Man*, so fascinatingly atmospheric.

5. Which major body of water in the Netherlands is famous for being reclaimed from the North Sea?

6. Can you name the ancient Assyrian and Babylonian temples that were shaped like terraced pyramids?

7. In 1964 this nation merged with Tanganyika to form the country of Tanzania.

8. Which Buddhist sect differs from traditional Buddhism by using introspection rather than the specified scripture? Name this sect and the scripture.

9. What is the name for a harem in India and Persia?

10. There is also a zygomatic process. Pray tell, what is it?

ZOUNDS AND ZYMURGY

answers

1. A zombie fulfills each of these definitions. It comes from the Congolese word *zumbi* (fetish).

2. These nifty threads were woven into the zoot suit.

3. ZIP stands for *z*one *i*mprovement *p*lan.

4. It is the zither, an instrument with 30 to 40 strings across a level soundboard. It is played with a plectrum.

5. The Zuider Zee is an arm of the North Sea. Through an amazing effort of willpower and engineering, it was controlled by dikes and much land was reclaimed.

6. It was a ziggurat (Assyrian: *zigguratu,* pinnacle).

7. Zanzibar joined this union. Previously, it was a 640-square-mile island off Africa's east coast. It also included Pemba Island.

8. Zen Buddhism differs with its own rituals, introspection, and intuition. The scripture, which they do not choose to use, is the Buddhists' Pali. This scripture is the Indic Prakrit, or dialect, which has become the religious language of Buddhism.

9. It is the zenana, the part of the house that is reserved for women.

10. This process is the bony arch on either side of the face just below the eye. There are a pair of quadrangular bones in the process.

TRIVIA FOREVER

As we near the destination of our trivia trek, the directions remain the unusual, the unique, and the bizarre. Here are more signposts to check with your analytical atlas.

1. Jack Benny's valet was named Rochester. What was Rochester's last name and which actor portrayed him?

2. Who uses the "tools of ignorance"?

3. How many of Vincent Van Gogh's paintings sold in his lifetime?

4. What area of the body is struck when hit by the controversial rabbit punch?

5. How many pounds does a keg of nails weigh?

6. There actually was a king who ruled his nation for fifteen minutes. Please name him and his country.

7. Which prominent rail line ran the super trains called "Locofocos" in the 1940s?

8. Millions like potato chips. Can you give their original name and the identity of the person who created this tasty snack?

9. Surely, there isn't a fish with lungs and gills—or is there?

10. In the definitive mystery, *And Then There Were None,* who invited the guests to the island of the doomed?

TRIVIA FOREVER

answers

1. His last name was Van Jones. The Rochester character was portrayed by Eddie Anderson.

2. The "tools" are a baseball catcher's equipment.

3. One of his paintings did sell in his lifetirne. It is called the *Red Vineyard*.

4. It is not a below-the-belt punch but, rather, a blow to the back of the neck.

5. A keg of nails weighs 100 pounds.

6. He was Louis XIX of France. On August 2, 1930, he assumed the throne and ruled for fifteen minutes. Then an opposing group of military men, legislators, business people, and clergy forced him to abdicate. He went into exile as a pampered royal anachronism.

7. None of them did. "Locofocos" was the nickname of the early version of friction matches in the 1830s.

8. They were called "Saratoga Chips" after their creation in 1853 at Saratoga Springs, New York. Most sources attribute George Crum, a cook at the Moon's Lake House restaurant in Saratoga, with originating them.

9. There certainly is. It is called the dipnoan (Greek: *dipnoos,* double-breathed). They are a small but resilient species found in several parts of the world.

10. Eight people and a housekeeping couple were invited to meet their fate by Mr. U. N. Owen. By saying his name quickly, you realize that their host was "unknown." However, the murderer did dwell among them.

TRIVIA FOREVER AND EVER

We've reached our journey's goal. Forsooth and behold! It is another fork in the trivia transit! Yes, for the curious of mind and the stout of heart, the trail of terrific trivia branches endlessly!

1. Who was radio's "All-American Boy"?

2. What is the name of the "whistle" song in the movie *The Bridge on the River Kwai*?

3. Can you describe what the words tabular, composite, star, and triangular have in common?

4. On what famous European raceway is the infamous Immelmann Turn?

5. Who might be the most likely to suffer from morning sickness while being the least likely to be pregnant? s

6. If fathers are considered to be their sons' direct predecessors, who was the next-to-the-last Mohican?

7. There really was a war that lasted less than an hour. Do you have any idea about the combatants and the duration of their confrontation?

8. The O.K. Corral was not the source of the term O.K. Can you trace its origin?

9. In the classic movie, *Champagne for Caesar*, the hero, Beauregard Bottomley, was on the quiz program called "Masquerade for Money." Beauregard missed the question worth $40 million. Do you know what that high-priced query was?

10. What was the correct answer that Beauregard Bottomley should have given?

TRIVIA FOREVER AND EVER

answers

1. He was Jack Armstrong. This hero was much admired by idealistic youths while many next-door girls swooned over his courage.

2. It is "The Colonel Boogie March." (It is a true lip-puckerin', knee-slappin', toe-tapper, too!)

3. They all are words for types of snowflakes.

4. This turn happens to be well above any road and the ground, too. It actually is an aerial maneuver that was first perfected by Max Immelmann, a German flier in the early 1900s. It involved a half loop and a half roll for a 180-degree change in direction.

5. The likely sufferer could be a husband whose wife is expecting and who is himself bothered by the symptoms of Couvade syndrome. This malady causes such husbands to believe that they are having pregnancy upsets like their expectant spouses.

6. He was Chingachgook, who was the father of Uncas. In the James Fenimore Cooper novel, Uncas was the last Mohican.

7. It was a skirmish between Great Britain and Zanzibar in 1896. In a time of volatile colonialistic rivalries and poor marksmen, very little damage was done to either side's gunners in 38 minutes. Fortunately, cooler diplomats prevailed.

8. It originated with the Democratic Club of Old Kinderhook, New York. Their first known meeting was on March 24, 1840. They used the term the "O.K. Club" for several years in various political events.

9. Beauregard Bottomley was asked to give his own Social Security number.

10. Neither Beauregard nor anyone else in the movie ever gave it. Beauregard's incorrect answer for his Social Security number was: 245-17-6012.

    P.S. The quiz show's audience liked him so much that the show's sponsor gave him his own radio program. By the way, he married the heroine, too. Yes, trivia certainly has its advantages!